International Relations

JOSEPH FRANKEL

International Relations

Second Edition

OXFORD UNIVERSITY PRESS
London   Oxford   New York
1969

Oxford University Press

OXFORD LONDON NEW YORK
GLASGOW TORONTO MELBOURNE WELLINGTON
CAPE TOWN SALISBURY IBADAN NAIROBI LUSAKA ADDIS ABABA
BOMBAY CALCUTTA MADRAS KARACHI LAHORE DACCA
KUALA LUMPUR SINGAPORE HONG KONG TOKYO

First published in the Home University Library
and as an Oxford University Press paperback 1964
Second edition, first published as an Oxford University Press
paperback 1969

Printed in the United States of America

Note to the Second Edition

AS THE TREATMENT is analytical, it can be left essentially un-changed after the lapse of four years since the first edition, apart from reference to major international events, up to and including the Czechoslovak Crisis in August 1968.

The major additions refer to the developments in the Cold War and in Chinese foreign policy.

J. F.

September 1968

Preface

WE CANNOT ALWAYS DRAW a clear distinction between domestic politics, i.e. politics within the state, and international politics, i.e. politics among states. Indeed, the most important issues, whether predominantly domestic or international, are not entirely either. For example, defence expenditure hinges largely on international insecurity but also on the funds available at home; wage policy affects primarily the pockets of the individual but has important repercussions on export prices and hence on the country's foreign trade.

As in life the two domains overlap, it is understandable that people trying to comprehend international affairs of which they have no direct experience or thorough knowledge, should resort to analogies from domestic politics. Here everybody is to some extent an expert: however uneducated he may be, he has some knowledge of the life and the traditions of his own country; he can reasonably guess the thoughts and reactions of his countrymen; through the mere possession of voting qualifications he participates in the political process. Unfortunately these analogies can be dangerously misleading; all the domestic expertise is of little use when applied to international affairs; in fact it can be outright misleading.

First of all, the study of the politics of other *states* presents considerable problems. We are all culture-bound, and persons quite well versed in the politics of their own country do not necessarily understand the politics of others, based as they are on different cultures and traditions; in fact they often disregard the differences or consider them as unnatural deviations from their own national norms. Even residents in a foreign country who are intimately acquainted with it, are often prone to misjudgements due to their different origin, as can be amply demonstrated by the views of many expatriates, the 'old hands', on the countries of their sojourn. Moreover, it is easy to forget how much points of view differ according to whether one is inside or outside the country. Citizens are naturally interested mainly in the domestic affairs of their country, while foreigners are equally naturally interested mainly in its foreign policy. It does not require much effort to imagine how different the resulting images are. Both the American 'capitalist' and the Soviet communist societies appear to be peace-loving to their own citizens who are impressed by domestic policies aiming at the attainment of economic and social goals; both appear aggressive to the citizens of the opposite number who think primarily of their foreign policies which are much less peaceful.

If it is hard to understand other states, it is even harder to understand *international society* as a whole. To start with, this society does not consist of individuals but of states. However sophisticated our approach might be, we still tend to be misled by linguistic usage and to consider states not as mental constructs, which they are, but as real entities. We *speak* about the relations between Britain and the United States as if they were relations between two persons and therefore we tend to *think* about them in the same way, even employing the simplified graphic images of John Bull and Uncle Sam. It is just as easy to slip into the error of considering the two countries as personified in their representatives, the President and the Prime Minister, or the Secretaries of State and of Foreign Affairs. The briefest reflection will indicate the dangers of forgetting the full implications of the artificial, conventional nature of states and of the important differences between persons acting in their official capacity and as private individuals.

Since the language of politics has been coined within the domestic sphere, its extension to international relations easily leads to analogies which are not fully warranted We speak of international society and of international organizations as if they were groupings of people; we discuss the international equivalents of law and morality; we discern the rights and duties of states; we analyse the organs of international institutions in terms

analogous to the traditional three branches of government. Needless to say all these analogies are defective. To a professional
lawyer international law is a very peculiar type of law; the
application to the behaviour of states of moral codes developed
for the individual incessantly breaks down; the ambiguities of the
concept of group rights are best demonstrated in the dangerous
effects of the principle of national self-determination, the international equivalent of the freedom of the individual; the comparison of the General Assembly of the United Nations with a
legislature, or of the Security Council with a government, makes
little sense, and even the less far-fetched analogies between the
United Nations Secretariat and a national Civil Service, or between the International Court of Justice and national courts,
should be approached cautiously.

These difficulties of institutional analysis are repeated in the
theory and philosophy of politics. Thinkers have been traditionally concerned mainly with state governments, with the relations between the individual and authority. Theories and philo-
sophies have been devised for a society of men which can be improved either through the improvement of its members, or of the
social order, or of both. They have only limited application to a
society of states where each member incessantly confronts other
intractable members and hence is concerned primarily with its
survival and is subject to the dictates of necessity. Many continental thinkers, from Machiavelli onwards, noted this fundamental difference, but on the background of their long tradition
of national security and of the 'moral opportunity' arising from
it, many British and American thinkers neglected international
relations.

Somewhat independently of the mainstream of political
thought, diplomatists and international lawyers developed a
common language, a set of common traditions with a specifically
international content, such concepts as balance-of-power, which
belong fully to the international sphere. Unfortunately, although
these traditions are still cherished by western diplomatists and
lawyers, their application is rather limited. International society
as we know it today has come into being only in the post-war
years: about half of its members, the Afro-Asian states, are
newcomers to the international stage, while the two Superpowers,
the United States and the Soviet Union, are newcomers to their

exalted status. Clearly categories and norms developed within the predominantly European context of the international society of the nineteenth century could scarcely be of general application today.

In our century, the growing popular interest in the relations among states has led to the development of a new specialized branch of knowledge usually described by the name earlier coined by Jeremy Bentham as International Relations. This new discipline is more than a combination of the studies of the foreign affairs of the various countries and of international history—it includes also the study of international society as a whole and of its institutions.

No theory of International Relations commands general acceptance and subsequent discussion is not based on any individual theory. However, in order to generalize about the relations of over one hundred and forty states, all different in size, power, and other attributes, and all acting against the backgrounds of their individual national traditions, it is necessary to have at least some working hypothesis or model. The difficulty lies in accommodating the conflicting patterns of international politics: it is impossible to deal with the subject without emphasizing either the role of the states or that of the international system; either conflict or co-operation;[1] either the clear but disappearing patterns of the past or the vague and merely hypothetical trends for the future.

The pattern of the past is still prominent. Mankind is loosely organized into an international society of sovereign states which have the monopoly of power and rely mainly, although not exclusively, on power in their mutual relations. These states are represented by individuals holding certain official positions who determine state policies under the complex, often conflicting influences and pressures from their domestic and international environments. Inevitably this international society is subject to repeated crises and to the constant danger of a major war, although the slowly growing co-operation among states gives some hope for an ultimate international order.

This hypothesis is neither particularly original nor profound, but it is useful and flexible. It not only provides a realistic

---

[1] J. Frankel, *International Politics: Conflict and Harmony*, 1969.

approach to the study of the 'behaviour of states' through that of the behaviour of their representatives but it also accommodates both the facts of the world of sovereign states governed mainly by power politics and the many phenomena of the contemporary world which cannot be fitted into its mould. It allows full scope for the co-operative trends which encourage hope for the order of tomorrow. Any reasonable treatment must be able to do that in order to do justice to our confused period when, as Sir Winston Churchill said, the past and the future overlap.

Contents

1
The States as Units of International Society

The Development of the State-System

MODERN STATES and modern international society are only a recent phenomenon. The three or four centuries of their history are only a small fraction of the more than 7,000 years of the recorded history of man and a proportionately smaller fraction of the half a million years of his biological history. Yet international relations were foreshadowed a long time ago.

The present state-system is explained in its broadest historical perspective by Aristotle's celebrated observation that man is by nature a political animal. At all stages of development people have needs and wants which they cannot realize alone, and hence they form social groups. Such groups vary greatly in their nature and scope, according to circumstances; but they invariably strike a host of organizational problems pertaining to the structure of the group, and also to its relationships with other groups, the equivalent of modern international relations. One fundamental problem here is that of delimitation, of finding the size best suited for the purposes of the group. Plato and Aristotle discuss it in their analyses of the Greek city-states; modern sociologists are concerned with it whether they develop theories of social communication or of areas of loyalty or of relations between the 'ingroup' and the 'outgroup'.

In fact something approaching international relations can be read into the social behaviour of animals which is now being reinterpreted by the zoologists. Groupings of animals are determined by considerations of biological survival; they must secure food and breeding grounds and hence are capable of fierce intra-species conflicts which generally revolve around the exclusive use of territory and the exclusion of trespassers likely to compete for the use of its facilities.

Most analyses of human organization start with an assumption about the original state of nature, describing it either as a state of innocence, a Golden Age, or as a Hobbesian war of all against all. For the purposes of this discussion it is unnecessary to decide in favour of either view. Whether man was originally motivated by sentiments of sympathy or of hostility, or by a mixture of both, he soon discovered that co-operation within a group provided bene-fits, and also that the contacts of his own group with other groups affected his interests, either positively or negatively. We can only speculate about the development of relations among primitive groups. Possibly, while they were few, men simply avoided contacts, but it is plausible to assume that with growing numbers and with increasing sophistication such contacts soon grew. If an analogy with the animal world suggests that the first contacts might have been hostile, already in pre-history some non-violent forms of inter-group relations were established and institutionalized (e.g. through heralds endowed with immunity) and mutually advantageous trade exchanges took place. Once such relations had reached a certain frequency and intensity, they became an important incentive to the organizing of an efficient central government to control them.

They required also some minimum conditions for intercourse between groups—some degree of linguistic understanding and probably also of religious community, sufficient at least to trust the oaths sworn by the other side. Thus the perennial dilemma of international relations faced man already in pre-history. When a group is no longer self-sufficient, when some of its vital needs can be satisfied only from the outside, is it preferable to ensure their satisfaction through the subjugation of the other groups involved or through some form of inter-group co-operation and exchange? The choice between war and peaceful co-existence is painful, since both carry their risks. Military conquest is the simpler method and, indeed, it seems to have been the rule throughout history, although we must allow for the likely tendency of the scanty early records to refer to the spectacular military feats of

rulers rather than to the unspectacular flow of peaceful intercourse such as international trade.

It is possible to interpret the political history of mankind as an
age-long series of attempts to determine the size of supreme social
groupings suitable for the circumstances of the time and the
place. While unifying forces led to empires based upon conquest
or to confederations based on consent, separatist forces invariably
reasserted themselves, causing the disintegration of the larger
units. Undoubtedly in many vital respects the whole globe has
now become one area of activity, but it does not necessarily follow
that the forces of unity will inevitably score a permanent victory.
Few people would accept today Sir Halford Mackinder's thesis of
geographical compulsion that 'the grouping of lands and seas,
and of fertility and natural pathways, is such as to lend itself
to the growth of empires, and in the end of a single World
Empire'.[1]

The nuclear menace, modern communications, economic inter-
dependence *could* lead to the integration of the world either by
conquest or by growing co-operation, but there is nothing inevitable about the process nor any assurance that, even if it succeeds,
unity would remain permanent.

The first large-scale political organizations, states, and state-
systems of which we possess records, developed about 5,000 B.C. in
the Tigris–Euphrates and Nile valleys and somewhat later in the
valleys of the great rivers of China. Their location was not due to
accident but to a social need common to all these areas. They all
required strong centralized organizations capable of constructing
and maintaining irrigation systems which were indispensable for
food production. Professor Karl Wittfogel has developed a plausible theory about the resulting despotic character of these societies
which he called 'hydraulic'.[2]

Growing numbers and sophistication were incessantly increasing the range of human needs and leading, although jerkily, to
larger human groupings. First in the valleys of the great rivers
and then in larger areas, states became enmeshed in networks of
inter-state relations alternating between the two patterns of
separate warring and co-operating units, and of great empires

[1] Sir Halford Mackinder, *Democratic Ideals and Reality*, 1909.
[2] K. Wittfogel, *Oriental Despotism: a Comparative Study of Totalitarian
Power*, 1957.

imposed upon them. These political systems, usually called civilizations, were fluctuating in their boundaries, but generally were
geographically segregated from one another, and each developed
a degree of cultural and political coherence. On the whole contacts among them were sporadic, although some were of great
cultural importance. The intrepid scholars, missionaries, and
travellers who crossed the formidable Gobi desert in the early
centuries of our era brought Buddhism from India to China;
oriental influences introduced by Alexander the Great altered
the character of Greek civilization; the 'barbarians' who worried
the Chinese and the Roman Empires were not only enemies of
these civilizations but also creative elements which became
assimilated to the former and rebuilt the latter in the form of the
medieval Christian Commonwealth; in our century anthropological studies of primitive people have opened our eyes to many
problems of our own.

In the eastern Mediterranean, civilizations interacted more
intensely and occasionally came into dramatic conflict. From the
unfortunate position of their small buffer-state between the
Assyrians and the Egyptians, the Hebrew prophets recorded the
clash between the two empires which began in the fourteenth
century B.C.; in the fifth century B.C. the Persians invaded Greece,
and in the following century Alexander invaded the Orient; the
Middle Ages witnessed a prolonged conflict between the Christians and the Moslems. Until the second half of the fifteenth
century A.D., however, Europe and the Middle East remained
almost wholly separated from the large organized civilizations in
China and in India as well as from the other, less organized
continents.

Our image of the international society of today as having arisen
mainly from the background of Western history is partly culture-
bound in its origins, but is of general validity. It is a historical
fact that owing to its superior technology and political organization, from the fifteenth century onwards European civilization
gradually extended its rule all over the globe. Today when other
civilizations and continents successfully assert themselves against
Europe, their own histories and traditions have assumed an obvious importance, but only as additions and corrections to the
existing system. Throughout the world, science and technology,
political institutions, culture-bearing languages, the very idea of a

society of sovereign inter-acting states, all have their origins in Europe.

Being an international society or system, international relations imply a multitude of units separate in some respects but in others constituting a whole—the result of an interplay between unitary and particularist forces. This interplay can be employed as an organizing device for the study of the rich and varied Western heritage; and the few subsequent paragraphs will indicate a way in which this can be done.

The Greeks, who devised the vocabulary of domestic politics, were less inventive for international relations, although they clearly distinguished some features which are characteristic of the modern European state-system, such as bipolarity and balance of power among sovereign states. While jealously preserving the independence of their city-states, they recognized a degree of unity in Greece as a whole and developed such common institutions as the Amphictyonic Council and the Olympic Games; they distinguished between conflicts within their own system (*stasis*) and wars with outsiders (*polemos*). The Romans epitomized the idea of unity in the ingenious institutions of their Empire which tolerated cultural divergences as long as they were not politically dangerous. The medieval Christian Commonwealth successfully, although not very effectively, preserved the *idea* of unity through the institutions of the Church, the Empire, and the Universities, while a chaotic multitude of local political units gradually combined into several hierarchically arranged feudal systems. The medieval order eventually crumbled down under the impact of the Renaissance and the Reformation.

With the disappearance of religious unity, particularist forces reasserted themselves. For a while both the Catholic and the Reformed Churches clung to the idea of medieval unity based on a common faith and endeavoured to impose their respective creeds on the whole of Europe. The local princes who rose to political importance through the accumulation and the ruthless use of power became immersed in religious wars, both fighting for their creeds abroad and trying to ensure their complete sway at home. As Machiavelli observed, modern states were based on power; however, their religious origin must not be neglected. Religious forces did not disappear from politics completely but, in the form of national churches, generally adapted themselves to the new units.

The resulting system of sovereign territorial states, which was formally established by the Peace Treaty of Westphalia in 1648, was at first limited to Europe. Gradually, however, European states extended their rule over other continents which they considered fair game for their expansion. In one sense, by including overseas territories within their empires, they spread the diversity of the European state-system over the whole globe. In another sense, they united the world physically, by opening communications, and culturally, by spreading European culture. Early in the twentieth century the system was threatened by several challenges. The empire-building process which was essential for the functioning of the European community came to an end when there were no more continents to annex and people to subjugate; Great Powers—the United States and Japan—arose outside Europe; under the impact of nationalism non-European peoples began to act more independently. Although still predominantly European, the inter-war international organization, the League of Nations, was, at least in concept, universal. The final blow to unity was caused by the gradual dissociation of the system from its Christian origins and by the split between the three offsprings of Western tradition—liberal democracy, communism, and fascism.

During its course, the Second World War was generally thought to be the defence of the system against its most dangerous adversary and, for some time afterwards, the forces for unity appeared to be on the march, admittedly not in favour of world-wide but rather of bloc integration. It seemed likely that the smaller states would become gradually absorbed into the orbits of the United States and the Soviet Union, the two Superpowers who had arisen in the wake of the war. The envisaged bipolar world has not materialized. The nuclear stalemate seems to neutralize the two Superpowers and to enable other states to assert themselves, whether they are uncommitted and neutral or under the influence of one of the two Superpowers. Instead of bipolarity based upon blocs integrated around the two Superpowers, a world-wide polycentric system has been gradually shaping, a system subdivided into western, communist, and uncommitted parts within which the separate state-units can act fairly independently. While the forces of unity have not prevailed within the blocs, they are operating, although in a very attenuated form, in the United Nations, which is world-wide.

In the last few decades, particularly since 1945, international society has undergone important changes, but its basic structure has remained the same since 1648, especially in theory; it is a society of sovereign territorial states. Consequently it is necessary to start with the analysis of the 'classical' international society and its member states and to postpone the discussion of evolution in this century. This approach emphasizes diversity, which is embodied in these states and has been prominent for the last three centuries. The forces of unity, however, have never fully disappeared and will be discussed in Chapters 6 and 7.

A word may be added about the implications of the highly dynamic nature of international society. Social forces operating within it change all the time in their nature but not in the mode of their operation. The metaphor of the swing of the pendulum is here quite illuminating, provided we accept that the swing changes from beat to beat both in its extent and in its speed. If we apply this metaphor to the interaction between the forces of unity and of particularism, the unity achieved under the Roman Empire meant that the pendulum reached one extreme position and then slowly, but in the last stages with catastrophic speed, swung to the particularism of the Dark Ages. The Holy Roman Empire constituted merely a feeble swing towards unity, and was again followed by the extreme particularism established at Westphalia. There is little doubt that the forces of unity have been building up since then, but the extent of the swing and its present momentum are difficult to ascertain.

Elements of Statehood

The member states are so prominent in international society that it is logical to start the analysis with them.

At the outset the fact must be stressed that states, being the most extensive units of human organization, are extremely complex. Hence they show quite different features when considered in their different capacities, as organizations of governmental authority in its relations with the citizens, or as economic, social, or cultural structures. By necessity the discussion of states in this context focuses around the role they play in international society; consequently many of their otherwise important characteristics can be barely touched upon or even mentioned.

Among the elements of the state structures those directly relevant for relations with other states must be mentioned first. A convenient starting point may be found in the formal legal approach. According to the British authority on international law, L. Oppenheim, a state '...is in existence when a people is settled in a country under its own sovereign government'.[1] This definition includes four distinct elements: a people, a territory, a government, and the characteristics of sovereignty.

The people. Since states are a form of social organization, this is obviously an essential element. The people are an aggregate of both sexes living in a community which need not be homogeneous. The size of the group is not fixed. There are over seven hundred million people in Communist China, while the people of the smallest states are counted in thousands. However, most jurists agree that there is some lower limit to the size of a people and they have doubts about the statehood of such tiny groups as Liechtenstein or Andorra, and deny the existence of conditions for a separate statehood of the smaller surviving colonial territories. Of course all these small groups are generally poorly equipped also in other essential elements of statehood.

The territory. Perhaps the most important characteristic of the modern state, distinguishing it from the medieval order, is its territoriality. This feature, sometimes described as impermeability or impenetrability, can be considered as the basic ingredient of the modern state: its strategic aspects are usually included in the analysis of state power, the political aspects are described as independence, and the legal ones as sovereignty.

The origin of the territorial state lies in the 'gunpowder revolution' which destroyed the security of the medieval castles and cities and resulted in a shift of the 'hard shell' of impenetrability from walls and moats to the broader confines of state boundaries. When neither local defences nor the Popes and Emperors could provide security, the princes, the rulers of larger territories, became its best guarantors and their states became the basic units.

[1] L. Oppenheim, *International Law*, vol. I, 7th edn., 1952.

We can consider the rise of the modern territorial state as a triumph of particularism over medieval unity, or as a partial victory of unity over the anarchy and disorder of the Middle Ages. On either interpretation, the modern territorial state is based on the twin elements of internal pacification and of external defensibility.

Territories of states vary in size as much as do their populations. The largest state in existence, the Soviet Union, covers an area of approximately 8·5 million square miles, but some states measure only a few thousands or even a few hundred square miles.

The government. The government consists of one or more persons who represent the people and rule according to the law of the land. Since all states conduct their foreign affairs through their governments, an anarchist community, even if it could exist on a sufficiently large scale, would not qualify as a state. The bolshevik revolutionaries tried to do away with their foreign ministry and to replace inter-governmental relations with direct relations with other peoples, but they soon gave up their futile attempt and their utopian 'withering away' of the state has not materialized. Governments play a crucial part in the making of foreign policy on behalf of their states, and hence their structures and mode of operation are discussed in some detail in Chapter 2.

Theoretically sovereign governments are in full control of the domestic and foreign affairs of their countries, but here, as on many other issues, a sharp distinction must be drawn between the two. As long as a government is recognized as such by other governments, it remains the legal representative of its country even if its control over it is severely challenged or completely lost. Thus the Nationalist Government of China is still recognized by the United States and by several other states as the Government of the whole of China despite the fact that since 1949 its rule has been limited to Taiwan and a few small islands; during the Second World War the governments-in-exile in London retained the recognition of Britain and the United States although they were temporarily divorced from the other elements of statehood. The obverse is likewise true—that groups organized as governments may be in actual control of a territory and yet remain unrecognized. Discrepancy between recognition and actual control leads to difficulties in international intercourse but may persist for a number of years. For instance, the United States does not recognize the Government of Communist China nor the incorporation, in 1940, into the Soviet Union of the three small Baltic states, Lithuania, Latvia, and Estonia.

Sovereignty. There are many definitions of sovereignty and much confusion is caused by the emotional content of the word, but there is general agreement that the sovereignty of states is important. Sovereignty has been described as 'the supreme political characteristic' or 'the central legal formula' of international society; its allegedly obsolete nature has been blamed for the major ills of contemporary international life.

In fact sovereignty expresses an important political reality, but is not absolute and does not necessarily impede the integration of states into larger units. Sovereignty means supreme authority which recognizes no superior and beyond which there is no legal appeal. This basic meaning has remained unchanged throughout modern times and Jean Bodin's definition made in 1576 that sovereignty is 'the supreme power over citizens and subjects unrestrained by law' has remained valid even though Bodin's sovereign absolutist ruler has now been replaced by the nation.

Again we must draw a distinction between the domestic and the international spheres because sovereignty gives rise to different problems in each. The classical problems of internal sovereignty such as the source and justification of the supreme power, its relation with the citizens, its location, and the question whether it can be divided, need not detain us long. In international relations sovereignty is accepted as a fact and governments are considered as representatives of their states, wherever political scientists and jurists might locate the ultimate sovereign power. External sovereignty can be divided, as shown by the historical cases of such 'semi-sovereignties' as protectorates, or the Free City of Danzig in the inter-war period, or the Free Territory of Trieste between 1945 and 1954, or by the still existing case of Monaco. In substance, however, in all these instances the semi-sovereign state has no supreme authority to conduct its foreign affairs, and hence is not really sovereign at all.

External sovereignty implies a basic contradiction to any notion of international order. A society of fully sovereign states is just as unthinkable as an anarchist society of fully sovereign individuals. Since law is the formal expression of social order, this contradiction shows most clearly in the relations between the institutions of the sovereign state and of international law.

International law establishes norms of social behaviour in the same way as does law within a state—or, as the lawyers call it, municipal law—but it is a much weaker kind of law precisely because its subjects, the states, are sovereign. International law is based on two apparently contradictory assumptions: first, that the states, being sovereign, are basically not subject to any legal restraint; second, that international law does impose such restraints. Obviously neither assumption is fully tenable. The state's external authority cannot be quite unlimited, otherwise there would be no law at all, nor can we expect the legal order to be centralized and strong. The principle of consent enables us to reconcile this basic contradiction, at least in theory. In the exercise of their sovereignty states can and do bind themselves to observe certain rules and contract certain obligations. Thus the rules of international law which they have accepted, explicitly or impliedly, do not derive from a superior authority above states, which would contradict their sovereign character, but are made by the states themselves. Consequently, international law is a law among states and not above them. Specifically, the states often agree to limit their sovereignty through the conclusion of innumerable international agreements and through their membership of international institutions.

Social Coherence and Nationalism

Some lawyers argue that a state exists as soon as the four formal elements can be found in it, and that recognition by other states merely recognizes this social fact. Others argue that such recognition is constitutive, that it is only through receiving such recognition that the state assumes its identity as a member of international society. On the former theory the formal elements are deemed sufficient; on the latter recognition is required in addition, in fact recognition is the most important element since it can be granted even if the formal elements are defective. Legal analysis does not, however, provide a full explanation. If we desire to understand how the elements are fused, what holds together the people under a government and ensures sovereignty, we must undertake a sociological investigation of domestic society.

The government organizes primarily the political life of the country and concentrates political power. Some of the newly established states have been recognized as such on the basis of this organization alone, although the social, economic, and cultural ties characterizing older states simply do not exist in them. It is, however, a historical fact that all states within the classical political system either started with or achieved such ties and that modern governments wield a considerable amount of not only political, but also economic and social power. Deficiencies in these non-political bonds must be taken into account when assessing the position and the prospects of the new states.

Even political power, which is the very basis of the recognition of the government by other states, cannot be taken for granted. The concentration of political power in the hands of the government is the rule, but not a rule without exceptions: it may be challenged by separatist forces, insurgents may arise and take over part of the state's territory, aggressors may occupy it, regional and minority allegiances may prevail against loyalty to the state. Especially with new states, we must check in every single case the extent of the actual political powers of the government; there are many examples of such powers being highly deficient.

Ever since the French Revolution nationalism has been the main spiritual and emotional force cementing all the elements of statehood in nation-states, and these have become the classical type of unit. Wherever the nation-state was a reality, nationalism buttressed and reinforced the state; where it remained an aspiration, nationalism endangered the existing multi-national units. Hence the relations between the state and the nation require careful consideration. The close historical links between the two concepts date back only just over a century and a half and we would not be justified in considering them as perennial. Unfortunately confusion arises from linguistic usage. Since the noun 'state' in English is rigid and precludes the formation of derivatives, we use substitutes formed from the more flexible word 'nation'. Thus international law and relations are the accepted terms for the law and relations among states; nationalization describes the acquisition of enterprises by the state. Although international law is the term used in other languages too, generally these languages are less rigid and they permit more accurate terminology such as *étatisation* or *Verstaatlichung* for nationalization.

Not only are states and nations not identical but the links between them vary greatly in time and place. Sometimes states precede nations, as in western Europe, sometimes nations precede states, as in central and eastern Europe; states of vastly different nature are multi-national, for instance the Soviet Union, Switzerland, and Malaysia; other states have large national minorities; some nations are divided into separate states, for instance the Germans, the Koreans, or the Vietnamese. Relations between the state and nation cannot be equated with those between the state and society because in no state is this society limited to the members of one nation alone, nor is any nation limited to the society within a single state.

If by a community we understand a social group within which men live all their lives, as distinct from associations within which they satisfy only some of their needs, a nation is a community. It differs from other communities first of all by size. The smaller communities, the family and the village, are small face-to-face groups, whereas a nation encompasses millions or at least many thousands. Second, the nation commands the supreme loyalty of its members; third, it has become closely connected with the institution of the state.

A nation can be defined either through the objective characteristics common to its individual members or through the subjective sentiments of these members, or through a combination of both. The 1939 Report on Nationalism produced by the Royal Institute of International Affairs found the following features in most—though not in all—nations:

1. The idea of a common government, whether as a reality in the present or the past, or as an aspiration for the future.

2. A certain size and closeness of contact between all the individual members. To take the example of contemporary Africa, tribes, however conscious of their distinctness, would not qualify for nationhood because they are too small, while Pan-African sentiments and contacts are too loose to constitute an all-African nation.

3. A more or less defined territory—here the Jews before the establishment of Israel are the major exception.

4. Certain characteristics distinguishing the nation from other nations and non-national groups. Language ranks high, although there exist some multi-linguistic nations like the Belgians or the Swiss, while some languages are shared by more than one nation, like English, French, German, or Serbo-Croat. Race, religion, and national character are among the most prominent of these common characteristics.

5. Certain interests common to all individual members. Especially through the instrumentality of the state, the nation has become the purveyor of most social needs; hence belonging to a nation means sharing many specific interests as well as the fundamental interest in the perpetuation of the nation.

6. A certain degree of common feeling or will, associated with a picture of the nation in the minds of the individual members.

According to subjective definitions, nationalism is a state of mind. In his *Representative Government* (1861) John Stuart Mill stressed common sympathies among members of a nation which 'make them co-operate with each other more willingly than with other people, desire to be under the same government, and desire that it should be government by themselves or portion of themselves, exclusively'. In 1882 in an oft-quoted passage, Renan spoke of the nation as a 'soul, a spiritual principle', whose existence is a 'daily plebiscite'.

Nations do not emerge as clear-cut entities from these definitions nor are they clear-cut entities in life. Thus in the inter-war period many German-speaking Austrians considered themselves as members of the German nation whereas few do so now; the Syrians and Egyptians think of themselves as separate nations while at the same time many of them regard themselves also as members of the Arab 'nation' which was, between 1958 and 1961, embodied in the ephemeral United Arab Republic; to choose an example closer to home, most Scots are conscious of their membership both of the Scottish and of the wider British nations, with various gradations of priority.

It would, of course, be possible to focus discussion on nationalism as the major spiritual force activating mankind, to analyse its role in filling the place previously occupied by religion or to speculate on the possibilities of its replacement by ideologies. It is, however, easier to understand nationalism if it is discussed as one of the features of the relations among states. Instead of trying to analyse the vague 'excesses' of nationalism we can more concretely explore the place of nationalism within the state-system.

The first point to be borne in mind is the historical fact that nationalism was generated on the Atlantic seaboard of western Europe, in France, England, Scotland, and Spain, and that it spread only slowly to the remainder of Europe and the western hemisphere, and only recently to the other continents. In the same way as socialism or trade unionism or any other idea or institution, nationalism means something different in different circumstances, and it has changed its meaning in the course of history. With its traditions stretching back for more than three centuries and within the homogeneous society of contemporary Britain, nationalism obviously cannot mean the same as it does in the Congo, where it appeared only a few years ago in a society torn by regional and tribal allegiances. Much of the confusion about the meaning of nationalism stems from unwarranted generalizations.

Second, following the indecisive conclusion of the wars of religion, nationalism became the most important element in state-making. In western Europe it legitimized and reinforced political structures which had previously come into existence; elsewhere it served as a powerful force to destroy existing structures and to establish new states roughly corresponding with nations. The emotional impact of nationalism remains unimpaired. It is possible to discover some signs of its weakening in western Europe, but the new Asian and African states are strongly nationalist. The rivals of nationalism have not been successful. The two World Wars in which workers rallied on the side of their own nations proved how wrong Marx had been in his expectation that the proletarians of all countries would unite, that class loyalty would prevail over national loyalty. On the contrary, nationalism has now been joined to socialism and has absorbed it. Likewise ideology merely reinforced nationalism in Fascist Italy and in Nazi Germany.

There remains the challenge of communism. Indeed, today ideological divisions cut across the bodies politic of such nations as the Germans, the Koreans, or the Vietnamese, and the ideologically determined 'iron curtain' is politically much more important than the boundaries between nation-states. However, these divisions are based not only upon ideology but perhaps even more on power relations between the Soviet Union and the United States, relations to which an analysis of the old-fashioned imperialism can be applied. Moreover, far from disappearing, nationalism reasserts itself and endangers the ideologically defined frontiers. In twenty years' time our period may appear to prove not the triumph of ideology over nationalism but rather the contrary, that political patterns cutting across nations are inherently unstable, however strong the supporting forces might be.

Even within the ideologically dominated Soviet bloc nationalism has raised its head in several countries, first of all in Yugoslavia, then in 1956 in Hungary and Poland, and lastly, in 1967 and 1968, in Rumania and Czechoslovakia. Chinese nationalism has prevented China's integration in the bloc and has led to a serious Sino-Soviet rift. In the Soviet Union itself, instead of merely tolerating nationalism, communism has since the beginning of the last war allied itself with Russian nationalism and has been trying, not entirely successfully, to submerge the other nationalisms in the Union in an all-embracing Soviet nationalism. Still, owing to its multi-national character and to the high proportion—about half—of the non-Russian nationalities, the Soviet Union is a unique case in which ideology rather than nationalism can be considered as the main social force cementing the state.

The Crisis of the Territorial State

After the final consolidation of the major states in Europe in modern times, states were considered stable, permanent units. To contemporaries, the elimination of Venice during the Napoleonic wars appeared to be daemonic. The disappearance of Poland as a result of three partitions at the end of the eighteenth century left a rankling question of Polish restoration which repeatedly disturbed international relations; other cases were few and of little importance. Today stability has disappeared. The present crisis of international society is due to a combination of causes: the proliferation of new states, inexperienced in the European traditions of international society and often unwilling to accept them;

the accumulation of power in the hands of the United States and the Soviet Union, two Powers relatively inexperienced in diplomacy and harbouring some strong reservations about Europe; but, most of all, to the crisis of the component units, the territorial states.

According to the cogent analysis of John Herz,[1] we are facing today a situation closely resembling that of the sixteenth and seventeenth centuries when the small medieval units were merging into modern states. As the gunpowder revolution had made the former inadequate for the needs of the day, so has the technological revolution of today rendered the territorial states obsolete. For some time the frontiers have been losing their meaning as lines delineating a territory under the complete sovereignty of its government. The first challenges were economic and psychological. Industrialized and hence no longer fully self-supporting states became extremely vulnerable to severance from external sources of supplies and markets. Psychological warfare was in evidence already during the French Revolution, and during the Napoleonic wars blockades proved quite effective. Then industrialization greatly increased economic vulnerability, while radio became extensively utilized for propaganda by all states. The main challenge, however, came from the technological developments in warfare, from the bombers, and even more from the nuclear weapons and the long-range ballistic missiles. The interior of the states, even of the Superpowers, has suddenly become 'soft', since it can be effectively struck from the outside.

With the ending of the impenetrability of the territory of states there disappears the very basis of their sovereign existence. Dependent as they are economically on other states, they are no longer self-contained economic units; having forfeited the hard shell of their frontiers which can now be so easily by-passed by propaganda and by military weapons, they are no longer suitable units of defence. Nevertheless, states are so firmly entrenched that they are likely to continue as supreme units of international society within the foreseeable future. It is difficult for man to enlarge his horizon and to accept a compass of loyalties broader than the customary one of his national state. Although increasingly less adequate for the purposes of foreign policy, in the last two generations states have amassed many additional powers in

[1] John Herz, *International Politics in the Nuclear Age*, 1959.

domestic affairs and have become the purveyors of many social needs hitherto left to private care. Finally, states remain the unquestioned guardians of national cultures and the political representatives of nations.

International society is now in a state of flux. States have so far retained their dominant position, but in order to meet the new challenges they have developed new institutional devices—coalitions, blocs, international organizations. In one way all these serve the purpose of buttressing the sovereignty of their members; but, in another way, they are further undermining it by becoming elements of international society in their own right and by pursuing their own interests or those of international society as a whole, as distinct from the individual interests of their members. There are two main types of these new groupings of states—regional and universal.

The regional groupings are of shorter standing but became conspicious in the post-war years when the communist and the anti-communist blocs gave the appearance of developing into two rival empires which would eventually divide the whole globe. Although the bipolarization did not materialize, institutions of great moment grew within the two blocs.

The North Atlantic Treaty Organization (NATO) is concerned with the defence of western Europe. It includes the United States, Canada, and their thirteen European allies, among them Great Britain. NATO constituted a departure from the traditional patterns of international military co-operation in that it was the first alliance to establish in peacetime a permanent integrated force under joint command. This force neatly solved the problem of German re-armament by including all the German forces and thus preventing the re-establishment of a national German force. Other members, however, retained most of their forces under their individual, national controls. Moreover, the strategic nuclear forces and the members' commitments outside, Europe, remained outside the scope of NATO. Thus it did not override the sovereignty of its members in defence matters though it circumscribed it to some extent. The Supreme Commander of the integrated force, invariably an American, is in direct command of some of their troops and they are committed in advance to a range of strategic decisions. Moreover, their national defence programmes are negotiated with the Organization at an early stage of their formulation and come up for discussion at the North Atlantic Council in December each year, thus influencing their national parliaments. Members do, however, often persist with their individual views and policies against NATO pressures; the ultimate decision is theirs and NATO has no provision for majority voting.

The evolution of NATO was slow and uneasy. The members' dedication was directly related to their fears of the Soviet Union and therefore NATO thrived under the impact of the Korean crisis but began to wilt when the Cold War abated. Its strategic provisions were never quite adequate for the defence of Europe as its members did not provide the minimum forces necessary for the defence of Europe in a conventional war whereas its place in the nuclear strategy became doubtful when the United States replaced its 'massive retaliation' doctrine by that of 'graduated deterrence'. There is no satisfactory doctrine for the employment of tactical nuclear weapons assigned to NATO by the United States and remaining under American control, and no institutional form has been found for incorporating a strategic nuclear component. Politically, NATO has managed to live with but not to resolve the problems of the preponderance of the United States within the Organization, or to arbitrate in the feuds between individual members, or to cope with the issues arising from the American, British, and French interests outside Europe, as manifested in the Suez Crisis in 1956 or in the Vietnam issue. By the mid-sixties, NATO had entered into a period of crisis which culminated in de Gaulle's withdrawal from all its military organs in 1966. Had it not been for the Soviet intervention in Czechoslovakia which revived NATO's original purpose, it may not have survived its twenty years' anniversary in 1969 which, according to the Treaty, opened it for revision.

Further-reaching are the three institutions of western Europe, the European Coal and Steel Community (E.C.S.C.), EURATOM, and the European Economic Community (E.E.C. or the Common Market). Their members are France, the Federal Republic of Germany, Italy, and the three smaller Benelux countries (Belgium, the Netherlands, and Luxembourg); the applications for membership made in 1961–2 and again in 1966–7 by Great Britain and by several other states were unsuccessful. The Communities bear a 'supranational' character, which means that, within their spheres of activities, they can actually make decisions which are binding upon members. Their central organs —now amalgamated—act on behalf of the Communities, but must obtain for important decisions the concurrence of the Council of Ministers, although within this Council decisions do not require unanimity. Consequently a member can be overruled, can be obliged even unwillingly to pursue a policy decided upon by the Community. Finally, in contrast to the customary time-limitation of treaties or the provisions for withdrawal, after an initial brief period, membership of the E.E.C. is permanent. The Communities are meant to be a step towards the political integration of western Europe, which, however, has not progressed very far in other fields.

At first the progress of the European Communities was slow and halting. The E.C.S.C. was established in 1951 as an avowed first step towards a European Federation, but its proposed successors, the European Defence and Political Communities, came to grief by 1954. The favourable market conditions and the great effort of the dedicated European 'integrationists' were the only reasons why the E.C.S.C. not only survived but was followed by the establishment in 1957 of the other two communities. The Communities then went rapidly from strength to strength, attracting Britain and the other reluctant outsiders to make unsuccessful attempts to join them. By the mid-sixties however, the communities reached a crisis. The boom was over and the economic growth slowed down; the communities became institutionally amalgamated but increasingly cluttered up by their own bureaucracy. Most importantly, grave political difficulties arose between France and the other members owing to de Gaulle's opposition to further progress towards supranational controls as well as to accepting Britain as a member. Like NATO, the European communities also reached a stage of acute crisis but, in contrast to it, their survival was not really in doubt.

Within the communist bloc, the regional institutions were never more than pale counterparts of the Western institutions. The Soviet Union had separate bilateral arrangements with Communist China which broke down entirely by 1962. In Eastern Europe, they established the COMECON as a counter to the Marshall Plan and the EEC, and the Warsaw Pact to meet the challenge of NATO. Both organizations merely served to institutionalize Soviet hegemony and did not prove really effective. From 1962 the Russians began to plan to endow COMECON with supranational powers in order to prevail against the persistent economic nationalism among its members and to slow down their individual attempts to improve their economic links with the West. The Warsaw Pact was mobilized only once, in August 1968, not for its avowed purpose of defence against NATO but to subdue and occupy one of its own members, Czechoslovakia, and to prevent her from developing an individual style of a liberalized socialist regime unacceptable to the Russians. Since the disbanding of the COMINFORM in 1954, there is no permanent institution in charge of the ideological direction of communist parties and states, but periodical international conferences of communist parties take care of that. They oscillated between stressing Soviet leadership and 'polycentrism', the idea that the national paths to communism may legitimately differ. In the early sixties they became a battlefield for the ideological struggle between the Soviet Union and China.

All these regional organizations are no more than extensions of existing states which enable them to survive, and, up to a point, they are also instruments of their powerful leaders. Universal international organizations, the United Nations and its Specialized Agencies, are more than that. They also are agencies which act on behalf of the international system as a whole, and they will be therefore more appropriately discussed in the latter context in Chapter 7. The United Nations and its collective security system do not, however, try to do away with the system of sovereign states. On the contrary, they can be considered as an attempt, admittedly not a particularly promising one, to perpetuate this system through a collective guarantee for all the member-states. Within the United Nations system the individual states are still most powerful. They try desperately hard to preserve their own sovereign positions, although they are often much less careful regarding the sovereign positions of others. It is unnecessary for our purposes to identify all the voting blocs operating in the General Assembly and to discuss their performance. It suffices to mention the existence of these blocs and the fact that on many issues states no longer take an individual stand but are governed rather by bloc considerations. The element that is least concrete, but nevertheless important in the United Nations,

is that of an international community. Although inter-governmental in form, and relying mainly on the support and actions of
its member-states, the United Nations has occasionally been acting on behalf of this community. Since, however, the greater part
of international relations still hinges around the actions of individual states, the machinery through which these states operate
must be analysed first.

Other Internationally Active Elements

There is a physical reason for the dominance of states in international relations: they are in control of the whole habitable
surface of the earth, and since any other organization must
operate somewhere, it must either acquire the control of a state or
become subject to one. Indeed, the history of mankind is full of
examples of such mergers, and often it is not quite clear whether
the state or the other grouping is predominant—it is possible to
consider communism as an instrument of state policy of the
Soviet Union, but it is also possible to consider the Soviet Union
as an instrument of communism; the Catholic Church in Spain
may be subject to the state, but, again, the state may be subject to
the Church. Without deciding on the merits of either interpretation, it is possible to agree that in all situations internationally
important organizations and groupings tend to merge with
states.

Nevertheless some trans-national organizations exist, and
although, until they identify themselves with states, they may not
be very important, they are by no means negligible. Churches are
the oldest and best known of these, especially the Church of
Rome, often referred to as the Vatican or the Holy See. Traditionally the Vatican has been treated as a sovereign state,
although its present territory is scarcely 200 acres, and for a while
it had no territory at all. The Vatican maintains diplomatic relations with well over forty states, not all of which are Christian,
and also hierarchical relations with over 400 million Catholics
scattered all over the world. By virtue of its spiritual supremacy
over the faithful, the Vatican can exercise political influence
over states in which these are a majority or a substantial minority.
Needless to say, difficulties sometimes arise, especially in relations
with communist states in which Catholics are treated with great

suspicion. The non-catholic Christian Churches, organized since 1954 into the World Council of Churches, do not play an analogous political part, nor do the other great religions. Buddhism has never had a central organization, Islam possesses none since the abolition of the Caliphate in 1923, nor does Judaism, despite its new spiritual centre in Israel.

Probably the most important trans-national elements are economic. At first the great trading organizations, like the English and the Dutch East India Companies, started as purely commercial ventures. They could not, however, conduct their trade without a degree of political control over their sources of supply, and their activities became increasingly political and military. After they had reached sufficient importance, the state invariably stepped in. The financial interests of the eighteenth and nineteenth centuries are epitomized in the fabulous Rothschild family. Between 1811 and 1816 the five sons of Amschel Rothschild established themselves as important bankers in five European financial capitals. While maintaining close links among themselves, they became providers of finance for their respective governments and, despite severe competition, their near-monopoly remained unimpaired for some three generations.

Then there arose the great industrial empires and corporations. Their interests extended beyond state-boundaries and became intermingled with state-policies. In the nineteenth century they could and sometimes did ask their national governments to acquire territory which they needed for supplies of raw materials or as markets. It is, however, a fallacy to attribute all imperialism to this factor, as Marxists do. In fact on many, perhaps most, occasions, it was the reverse; the governments used economic interests in order to promote national expansion. The corporations had the alternative of straight competition with their foreign rivals, but this was hindered by governmental restrictions on free trade and often was not very profitable.

The usual solution was found in co-operation through international cartels, but these again were sometimes used by states for political purposes. For instance the cartel arrangements between German and American firms in the inter-war periods in chemical, light metal, and plastics industries, succeeded in preventing the production of strategically essential materials in the United States because there were more profitably obtained in Germany.

Only when the war broke out did the Americans realize to what extent their military potential had thus been weakened.

Giant corporations today maintain direct relations with foreign governments through their equivalents of foreign ministries and ambassadors. Especially prominent are the seven giant international oil companies, including Royal Dutch Shell and British Petroleum (previously Anglo-Iranian), Unilevers, Krupps, or the companies representing American interests in copper in Chile, in sugar in the Dominican Republic, in fruit in the so-called 'banana-republics'. On the whole these corporations operate independently and do not seek government protection except in the cases of nationalization of their foreign establishments, which have become frequent since 1945. Government protection is not, indeed, of much avail, as is shown by the losses sustained by British oil interests in Persia in 1952, or by the American sugar interests in Cuba in 1961. Sometimes governments intervene in the policies of the corporations, and, having the ultimate power, are obeyed. Thus American Administrations successfully restricted trade with Nazi Germany in 1940–1, and prevailed on the American oil companies to refrain from purchasing or carrying nationalized Persian oil in 1952. The industrial empires, however, are not fully subservient. Even in wartime some trade with enemy states continued and the trade restrictions directed against communist countries and against Rhodesia are often avoided.

For a while Marxists expected that the clarion call for the proletarians of all countries to unite would spell the end of national boundaries, but the First World War, in which the majority of the socialists in the various countries rallied behind their national governments, ended this illusion. The several successive Socialist Internationals did not have much impact on inter-state relations. Their communist successors were international only in form; the inter-war Comintern, which organized the communist parties throughout the world, was under the Russian thumb and served as an instrument of Russian national policy; even more so was its more limited post-war successor, the Cominform, which was formally disbanded in 1954. Other political internationals such as the liberal one, or organizations of Eastern European Exiles, have no great political significance.

International trade union federations are another offspring of the Marxist idea of the international solidarity of workers, although, as is obvious in Britain and openly avowed in the United States, trade unions have become fully nationalized and are mainly concerned with obtaining bigger slices of the respective national cakes. The two mammoth international organizations which have come into being since the war, the communist-dominated World Federation of Trade Unions (W.F.T.U.) and the western-dominated International Confederation of Free Trade Unions (I.C.F.T.U.) are engaged less in asserting internationally distinctive trade unionist interests, than in supporting their respective sides in the cold war, particularly in competing for influence over the politically important trade unions in the new states.

2
The Making of Foreign Policy[1]

The Process and the Constitutional Machinery

IT IS CUSTOMARY to personify states and to speak of 'British foreign policy' or 'British decisions', but in fact these are not made by the state but by single individuals and groups who act on its behalf. Theirs, like all other human activities, can be considered in terms of interaction between the decision-makers and their environment.

Most human needs and desires cannot be satisfied without some form of action, and this is generally preceded by a decision, meaning an act of will determining in one's mind the course of action to be taken. Decisions and resulting actions are the product of a confrontation in the minds of the decision-makers of their wants and desires with what they know about their environment. It is this psychological environment, the *image* of reality that people hold, which plays a part in their decisions, however much such image may deviate from the environment as it really is.

The fundamentals are identical, but decisions taken on foreign policy differ from those taken in other fields in that they are subject to a unique interplay between domestic and foreign environments. The persons involved occupy certain official positions of trust and importance empowering them to act on behalf of their society in its external relations. It is the values of this society which they are to uphold; it is the interests of this society which

[1] This chapter condenses part of the argument in *The Making of Foreign Policy* (1963) by the author.

they represent. When, however, they engage in their jobs, they are confronted by statesmen and officials belonging to other domestic societies and pursuing their own values and interests. Thus the international environment often proves intractable; statesmen sometimes face insuperable obstacles when pursuing the interests of their respective countries, and they are constantly subject to pressures which are at variance with domestic pressures.

Political life does not invariably conform to legal rules determining competence, but in the making of foreign policy the *formal* decision-makers are particularly important. Governments on the whole fully monopolize the control of foreign policy. This is partly due to the historical traditions dating from the absolutist period, and partly to the logic of the present situation, in which, as a rule, governments alone deal with other governments, command the best sources of information, and have the monopoly of legitimate and a near-monopoly of physical force. Any influence on foreign policy coming from other sources must be exercised through governments.

Although domestic political systems greatly vary from country to country and from period to period, certain uniformities do exist. The head of state does not usually play an effective part in foreign policy and his participation is mainly ceremonial. Exceptions can be found only in countries where the head of the state combines executive functions with his office—as the Presidents of the United States or of the Fifth French Republic. Powers are concentrated in the hands of the government, or, as the Americans call it, the executive, and within it, in the hands of its head and of the minister of foreign affairs (in Britain called the Secretary of State for Foreign Affairs or Foreign Secretary for short, in the United States called the Secretary of State). Other elements which should be taken into account are legislatures; the civil servants in the foreign ministry and in certain other, for the purposes of foreign policy, subsidiary departments; and public opinion. All these will be considered in turn.

The Head of the Government and His Foreign Minister

The head of the government usually plays a decisive role. In the presidential system in the United States the members of his cabinet are merely his advisers and, although this is somewhat oversimplified, it is fundamentally true, as ex-President Truman remarked, that 'the President makes foreign policy'. In Britain major policy decisions are generally taken by the Cabinet as a whole, but the Prime Minister is fairly free in the choice of its members and leads its deliberations. Moreover, we have on record several important instances when the Prime Minister did not consult the Cabinet as a whole on major foreign policy moves; the Suez expedition in 1956 is a case in point. He is normally sure of the loyalty of his Cabinet colleagues and of the support of his party members in parliament; provided his parliamentary majority is reasonable, his power is secure. This is not so with coalition governments, such as that headed by Winston Churchill during the last war.

The head of the government generally chooses a foreign minister to his liking, but sometimes he may be restricted by party priorities or coalition requirements. The minister is subordinate, but when the head of the government lacks any special interest in foreign policy and fully trusts him, his may be the decisive voice. This was quite recently the case with Ernest Bevin in the Attlee Governments in Britain and, to a lesser extent, with John Foster Dulles in the Eisenhower Administrations in the United States. The modern tendency, however, is for the heads of government to assume personal responsibility for major foreign policy decisions; occasionally they combine the two offices despite the crippling amount of work involved. In any case, they are personally involved in the so-called 'summit meetings' which have been made possible by modern communications.

Even when personally conducting foreign policy, the head of the government cannot help leaving large areas of activity to his minister. When the views of the two are closely related, no serious problems of co-ordination arise, but where they diverge, in time the head removes the minister from office or by-passes him by using other ministers or personal agents.

In the Soviet Union and in other communist states, real power is vested in the communist parties rather than in the traditional governmental machineries which they all possess, though it is possible to exaggerate the unimportance of the latter. Undoubtedly the First Secretary of the Communist Party is the key figure, even if he does not combine his office with that of the president of the council of ministers, as, for a while, both Stalin and Khrushchev did. While Stalin was omnipotent within the Party, his successors have to tolerate opponents and depend on decisions taken by their colleagues, admittedly those in the Politburo rather than in the Council of Ministers. Their position differs in degree rather than in kind from that of the heads of government elsewhere.

Legislatures

Discussion here must be limited mainly to the western democracies since, with the partial exception of India, parliamentary institutions, when they exist elsewhere, do not wield real powers.

Parliamentary powers are generally smaller in foreign than in domestic affairs, but even so they can be important. They vary from country to country and they are determined by an interplay between fairly stable constitutional arrangements and such more ephemeral elements as the political climate, the strength of the parties, and the characters of the leading personalities. One extreme can be found in the United States where the principle of 'checks and balances' and the absence of party discipline ensure the Congress a role co-ordinate with that of the executive, the other in the Soviet Union where the Supreme Soviet lacks any effective powers; other systems lie somewhere in between.

Being large and clumsy bodies, parliaments cannot effectively initiate foreign policy and are limited to the exercise of the power of veto over policies proposed by governments. Their main legal power usually lies in the ratification of treaties. In a particularly stiff form, the American constitution requires the concurrence of a two-thirds majority of the Senate. This led to repeated rejections of treaties which culminated in the refusal to ratify the Peace Treaty of Versailles in 1919 but, since then, improved methods of consultation, bi-partisanship, and the employment of 'Executive Agreements' have rendered the Senate's powers much less formidable. Also in a multi-party system refusal of ratification can have serious effects; for example, in the Fourth French Republic parliament threw out the European Defence Community Treaty in August 1954. The House of Commons lacks legal powers of ratification, although it has the opportunity to debate important treaties which, under the convention of the so-called

'Ponsonby Rule', lie on the table for three weeks before their ratification by the government.

All legislatures which exercise real power hold the purse-strings, and governments depend upon them to allocate the funds required for foreign policy. This is a telling power today when defence expenditure usually constitutes one of the main items of the budget and foreign aid is widely given. It is the reason why the House of Representatives is becoming increasingly important in the making of American foreign policy. Parliaments are also required to pass any laws which may be necessary to implement international treaties.

Legislatures can go beyond that and continuously control foreign policy through their standing committees. This has happened particularly in the United States where such committees employ staff independent of the Executive, are constantly consulted by the State Department, and conduct investigations and hearings. The Chairman of the Senate Committee on Foreign Relations occupies a key position which, at times, may be more important than that of the Secretary of State. The House of Commons has not established a standing committee, in order to avoid the inevitable consequence of sometimes embarrassing the Foreign Office and of depriving it of much of its flexibility. It exercises only intermittent control through extensive foreign policy debates and also through questions put to the Government at question-time.

Civil Service

An important distinction is usually drawn between policy-making and administration. In theory the ministers make the policy while the officials merely execute it, but it is scarcely possible to exaggerate the importance of the bureaucratic machinery. Its members preserve the continuity of policy, while foreign ministers of different parties and views come and go. Moreover, these ministers—and also heads of government—usually rise to power on the basis of their achievements in the field of domestic politics; when they assume their responsibilities for foreign affairs, they naturally become dependent on expert advice.

It is difficult and somewhat futile to decide to what extent a minister makes decisions or merely confirms decisions made by his officials. This is only of academic interest when they do not differ in their views; when they do, the politicians generally prevail, though only in the long run. In Fascist Italy and in Nazi Germany the permanent officials who rejected or only half-heartedly accepted the policies of their masters were by-passed and eventually removed; in Britain, when Neville Chamberlain clashed with the Foreign Office over his policy of appeasement, he removed Lord Vansittart from his powerful position of Permanent Under-Secretary and continuously by-passed diplomatic channels, using for the purpose his personal agent, Sir Horace Wilson.

Nevertheless, where policies are less firm and clashes less pronounced, the advice of the officials carries much weight, and, if it is ignored, the implementation of policies contrary to their views may be slowed down or even actively obstructed. The ingrained attitudes of the permanent officials should be neither minimized nor exaggerated. It is unlikely that a British Foreign Secretary would succeed with a pronouncedly pro-Israeli policy against the pro-Arab traditions of the Middle Eastern Department; the Foreign Office tradition of giving only lukewarm support to international organization and, until 1961 at least, of lack of sympathy with European integration, may have strongly contributed to British policies in these fields. On the other hand, the French Foreign Ministry must have gone through a fundamental reappraisal before embarking on the policy of integration with Germany. Bureaucracy is particularly prominent in France, where it provides the main element of continuity in the constant change of constitutions and governments. In Germany, it has survived the war as one of the least affected centres of power and has been confirmed in its traditional importance by the occupation authorities, but apparently the average German official remains indifferent to politics beyond his narrow specialist domain. Little information is available about the secretive working of Soviet bureaucracy. In terms of power, the Soviet equivalent of western foreign ministries is probably the Foreign Department of the Central Committee of the Communist Party, the various sections of which maintain close relations with the corresponding sections of the Foreign Ministry. Stalin's personal secretariat or the so-called 'technical cabinet', an institution perpetuated by Khrushchev and his successors, probably still continues to play a central part in Soviet domestic politics and, in all likelihood, influences also the determination of foreign policies.

The enormous increase in the scope of international relations has led to the blurring of the traditional demarcation lines between domestic and foreign affairs. Despite the fact that foreign ministries are now grossly overworked, most other departments are involved in many foreign issues, giving rise to grave problems of co-ordination. The situation is most acute in the United States owing to its transition from the restrictions of isolationism to the expansion of world leadership. In 1949 no less than forty-five out of the identified fifty-nine departments, commissions, boards, and inter-departmental councils were involved in some aspects of foreign affairs. In Britain eight ministries were seriously and continuously concerned in the negotiations with the European Economic Community between 1956 and 1958; presumably all these departments were involved also in the negotiations in 1961-3 and 1966-7. While co-ordination in Britain is undertaken through informal contacts and through Cabinet Committees, in the United States it has led to a confusing proliferation of bodies and to the employment of various methods, none of which has been really successful.

Soviet experience is characteristic of the problems involved. Until recently Soviet foreign policy, which is rigidly controlled by the Party, was much better co-ordinated than are foreign policies in the West. Since the last war, however, the Soviet Union has intensified and ramified its foreign relations—there are intimate links with other communist countries, massive foreign aid, delicate relations with the new, uncommitted countries, increased cultural and commercial exchanges with the west. Despite strict central control, difficulties of co-ordination at middle and lower levels are likely to arise. For instance, when the poet Pasternak was refused permission to accept the Nobel Prize, the decision, apparently handled as a domestic matter, amounted to a major blunder of foreign policy.

The administration of foreign affairs is partly decentralized since states maintain diplomatic missions in the capitals of all other states with which they have relations of any intensity or importance. Before the development of modern communications, diplomats in charge of missions could not receive prompt instructions from their ministries and were often forced to make major decisions on their own responsibility. Today this is rarely necessary, but foreign envoys are much more than mere subordinates following instructions. Not only do they supply and interpret information from the country of their sojourn but they can still be called upon to make a prompt decision on the spot if faced with a sudden minor emergency.

Subsidiary Services

Foreign policy is not conducted by diplomacy alone; it relies heavily on the military forces and on the scientists who supply them with up-to-date weapons, on economists, and also, especially today, on intelligence and propaganda services. Absolutist rulers of the past could personally deal with all these matters, but now such integration is unthinkable and extensive specialized services have been developed. These services are generally merely subsidiary to diplomacy but in some circumstances they can exercise great influence upon the decision-making process—the military when it comes to securing bases, strategic frontiers or allies; the scientists concerning the development of weapons; the intelligence services when they act without full governmental control or diplomatic guidance.

Of these, the military are by far the most important, although civilian control is the rule both in the West and in Communist countries and is considered as an ideal even in the remaining countries where military dictatorships tend to represent themselves as mere stepping-stones towards civilian government. Of all the industrialized countries, it was only in Germany and Japan that the military developed fairly independently of civilian control, but in neither have they recovered their independence since the last war.

Naturally, strategic and diplomatic considerations do sometimes clash, especially in wartime, but although the civilians can ignore military advice only at their peril and hence do not reject it lightly, they do so when it seems to them expedient. Matters are further complicated today by the policy of deterrence, in which the weapons are not supposed to be *used*, but only to deter. Hence success depends on *what* weapons are available, and this is in the hands of the scientists, and not only on how they are to be used, which is the traditional subject-matter of military strategy.

In the period since 1937, after the potentialities of nuclear energy had been finally ascertained, some nuclear scientists did, indeed, try, though unavailingly, to interfere in politics to prevent the use of bombs against Japan and to bring them under international control. Their advice on new weapons and on the likely achievements of the rival Power, advice inevitably coloured by their political views, undoubtedly affects policy decisions.

Aid-administering agencies play a minor part in countries offering foreign aid, particularly in the United States, where they have been partly but never fully subordinated to the Department of State. Similarly subordinate are the propaganda services, despite the great sums of money lavished upon them by all major Powers. More independent are the intelligence services, which tend to engage in cloak-and-dagger activities and pursue them beyond the mere collecting of information. The United States Central Intelligence Agency was conducting a foreign policy of its own for a number of years. It was responsible for the support of Chinese nationalists in Northern Burma, the U-2 reconnaissance flights over Soviet territory, the invasion of Cuba in 1961, and the encouragement of the right-wing government, established with its support in Laos, to resist coalition-government plans sponsored since 1961 by the Department of State. Apparently President Kennedy, who was seriously affected by its blunders, decided to impose a closer check on its activities. It is difficult to identify the impact of the highly diversified Soviet intelligence services but undoubtedly these, as well as the services of other major Powers, operating as they do in secret and with substantial funds, have ample opportunities for at least an occasional independent action.

Public Opinion

It is unnecessary to postulate a democratic ideology or a theory of the 'general will' in order to acknowledge the ultimate importance of the people as a whole. As David Hume noted, 'It is ... on opinion only that government is founded; and this maxim extends to the most despotic and most military governments as well as to the most free and most popular.' Public opinion comes to bear as an unorganized whole, in the form of a 'mood', which prescribes the limits within which policy can be shaped, and also through organized sectional interests and their leaders and inter-mediaries. Until 1914 public opinion was only marginally in-terested in foreign policy, but during the later stages of the war the rapidly growing labour force began to insist on its popular control, as a key to a liberal peace. The new force was vulnerable to outside influence and was appealed to both by Wilson and by the Bolsheviks; the internationalists regarded it as the great weapon which would ensure peace.

This new element in the conduct of foreign policy has given rise to a host of problems most of which still remain unsolved. The people are generally poorly informed and, even if informa-tion is available to them, their judgement is often wrong. Here opinions vary—radicals tend to attribute some wisdom to the man in the street, while thinkers less radically inclined, especially practising diplomats, generally deprecate his powers of under-standing. While the former favour more information for the public, the latter are inclined to withhold it on dangerous mat-ters and to manipulate it in the direction desired. This ties up with the problems of guidance. The idea of democracy does not imply that the leaders should rigidly follow public opinion, but it does imply and sometimes even demands, that they should direct it.

It is not always easy to know the reaction of public opinion to any given issue. This is so even in Western democracies where the people's views are generally fairly articulate and are frequently ascertained in free elections and through public opinion polls. On an issue as important as that of Britain joining the Common Market, at the crucial moment in August 1961, when the government decided to apply for membership, the state of public opinion simply could not be guessed; the various sec-tional interests had not yet adopted a firm stand and the general public was completely ignorant of what was involved. Opinion became fully clarified as being favourable only during the second application in 1967.

In countries where political life has achieved a certain degree of sophistication, public opinion is structured and organized in political parties and pressure groups. Only a small proportion of the citizens may be interested, informed, and active in foreign policy matters, but those who are, assume positions of leadership at various levels. Their opinions are indicative of the way in which public opinion is likely to react and they are the most promising people upon whom influence can be brought to bear. They are more influential than the popular press and other mass media, important as these are, in influencing public opinion.

In the rigidly governed communist countries public opinion is not structured from below, as in the West, but organized from above, through a hierarchy of leadership. Here the extensive agitation-propaganda apparatus used for the purposes of discovering and manipulating public opinion has apparently been only partially successful.

In the well-integrated British and Western European societies, emotional appeals by a Mosley or a Poujade find little hearing, but in the somewhat less integrated United States, Senator Joseph McCarthy was for a while a dangerous demagogical leader. In the many societies where political structures are rudimentary, the illiterate masses of unskilled and often unemployed urban workers are unstable in their recent divorce from their rural origins and unhappy in their wretched living conditions, while the students are aware of the shortcomings of their societies but are incapable of providing a rational or practical answer to their problems. Here radical nationalists and communists have great scope for demagogic appeals.

National Interest and National Values

'National interest' is the key concept in foreign policy. In essence, it amounts to the sum total of all the national values—national in both meanings of the word, both pertaining to the nation and to the state. This concept is rather vague. One common-sense definition describes it as the general and continuing ends for which the nation acts. It is thus characterized by its non-specific nature, by a degree of continuity, and by its connection with political action. A major ambiguity arises from the use of the concepts in different contexts without sufficient clarification. National interest can describe the aspirations of the state; it can be used operationally, in application to the actual policies and programmes pursued; it can be used polemically in political argument, to explain, rationalize, or criticize. The recurrent controversies on foreign policy often stem from these ambiguities and not only from the different ideas about what national interest may indicate.

National interest need not be so narrowly defined as to exclude moral, religious and other altruistic considerations, but, to be effective, these must have been accepted as part of it. In actual practice it may not always make much difference whether a decision is made by a statesman who subscribes to the Hegelian theory that the state is the supreme good (which is the foundation of totalitarianism) or by another who believes that the state is merely an instrument to satisfy the needs of the citizens. As long as the state remains responsible for the welfare of its citizens in most avenues of life and the purveyor of many social needs, both may interpret national interest in a similar way. They may, however, greatly disagree in the future as more human needs have to be satisfied outside the confines of the state. A narrow interpretation of national interest, based upon the idea that the state and its sovereignty must be preserved at all costs, would indicate a different general attitude to international organization than a liberal one based upon the idea that only such organization is capable of meeting some important needs.

All statesmen are governed by their respective national interests, but this does not mean that they can never agree on anything. On the contrary, they often do, but only on the basis of their conceptions of these national interests. If a statesman agrees to concessions, he does so only when he is convinced that this brings some advantage to his state, directly or indirectly. For instance, the favourable treatment of the trade of another country may secure not only trade-openings but also friendship; support for a partly obnoxious international institution may be worth while in order to secure the continuation of its useful activities or to ensure international good will. Co-operation is conditional upon the existence of a suitable framework, of a reasonably stable international order within which the actions of other states are predictable and therefore rational foreign policy is possible. From here stems the interest of all states in this international order, again according to their national advantage. If they find this order congenial, they support it and, if necessary, defend it; if uncongenial, they endeavour to alter it accordingly.

At least for the time being, no alternative to one's own national interest is conceivable. If a statesman were to give his allegiance to the national interest of another country this would be treason, and treason is extremely rare at the very top level of authority. If his first loyalty were to international organization rather than to his own state, he would be unlikely to rise to a position in which foreign policy decisions are made. On a liberal interpretation of national interest, clashes between national and international loyalties can usually be avoided, but if one does occur, the statesman's first duty is to his state.

The notion of national interest is based upon the values of the national community, values which can be regarded as the product of its culture and as the expression of its sense of cohesion, values which define for men what they believe to be right or just. The relationship between these values and concrete policy objectives requires some explanation.

Values belong to the realm of 'the ought' and may or may not be translated into concrete political objectives. To say that the rulers of the Soviet Union are adherents of the communist ideology means that they believe that communism ought to prevail throughout the world, but not necessarily that they are actually pursuing concrete objectives to achieve it. The historical fact that communism has been expansive throughout its existence indicates that the rulers actually do pursue such objectives, but a person wishing to analyse Soviet foreign policy should examine the question whether concrete objectives remain intact after such events as Stalin's death. To say simply that, because communist ideology makes the spread of communism desirable, therefore the communist leaders automatically pursue appropriate expansionist goals, may debar us from noticing a possible change in these goals. With equal profit, the communists could abandon their confusion between our desire to get rid of communism (which is, indeed, an important element in western ideology) and the aggressive strategic objectives which they impute to us, to achieve this in practice.

Usually value-systems are loose and they often include conflicting values; on any concrete issue the problem arises how to find out which values apply. A case in point is trade with Communist China. The British think of it mainly in terms of achieving the maximum trade possible while the Americans are more concerned with the danger of strengthening a potential enemy; the issue is predominantly economic for the former but predominantly political for the latter. To make things worse, states-men may be deliberately misleading in what they say; according to Freud, they may themselves be ignorant of their true motiva-tions. Finally, different cultures do not attribute the same im-portance to the same values; there is, for instance, little meeting ground between a westerner who stresses economic values and a non-European who refuses to do so.

Throughout the history of political thought man has been seeking a supreme value which could be used as a general yard-stick. Unfortunately the very fact that so many conflicting theories have arisen casts some doubt on the general validity of any one of them. The popular yardstick of national interest is too vague and that of power is insufficient. Power has, in fact, been the necessary condition of self-preservation, and a state which ignores this condition persistently cannot escape the danger of disappearing. This does not mean that the yardstick is or can be persistently applied to all values in all situations; indeed, it is sometimes ignored and even deliberately acted against.

Whenever two or more values clash, the relative importance of both must be weighed and established, even if there can be no agreement on the identity of a supreme value. This 'ranking' of values is not easy because intensity fluctuates from case to case and is often determined by emotions. For example, a violation of national frontiers by a small detachment of an unfriendly neigh-bouring state may be considered as an unpleasant but purely local incident or it may be blown up to a symbolic issue warrant-ing retaliation, even to the lengths of waging war. In short, it is quite impossible to develop a rational 'value calculus' and choices among values are bound to remain largely intuitive.

Values in their Interaction with the Environment

Values reach their full political significance only in action, when the statesman actively applies them to his image of the environment. In the vaguest and most general form this leads to what may be described as a vision of the good life, an arrange-ment of the elements of reality—as perceived by the decision-maker—to approximate as closely as possible to the values he holds. Needless to say when it comes to actual action, the vision can never be fully realized because the environment is always, at least to some degree, intractable. There is always some tension between the vision of the good life and life itself even when the vision is so moderate that it can be easily translated into a concrete political programme. Some visions are quite utopian, completely unrealizable, and most of them contain a sizeable utopian element.

While the vision of the good life indicates only the general direction desirable for foreign policy, more specific principles of behaviour are deduced from it and, most importantly, also concrete political objectives—or ends or goals—which the statesmen decide to pursue. The decision of how far they are prepared to go in their efforts to secure the values, may be called the pitching of the level of aspirations. This level differs with the personality of the individuals and with national character which can be either predominantly optimistic, determined, ready to take risks, or predominantly pessimistic, cautious, preferring to play safe. It fluctuates also according to how successful action proves to be.

To arrive at a political decision, a statesman must juxtapose his values and his environment. Hence we must investigate how he arrives at his knowledge of this environment. The major link here is information, and indeed, all foreign ministries and, within their specialized fields, also military authorities, assiduously collect it. However abundant, the open and legitimate sources of information are generally deficient on the most important matters and have therefore been traditionally supplemented by espionage.

Although top-level statesmen have full access to the information available to their governments, they cannot possibly digest it all. By the time information reaches them it tends to become condensed and separated from reality to the point of allowing complete misinterpretation. This being so, skilful politicians can and often successfully do use their intuition. Personalities differ immensely in this respect. In recent American history we may contrast President Eisenhower, who refused to become acquainted with facts directly and relied on John Foster Dulles to bring to his attention anything of real importance, with the voracious appetite for information and the extraordinary range of Presidents Franklin D. Roosevelt and John F. Kennedy.

In order to select what is relevant from the bewildering variety of facts and events, one must have some criteria of relevance.

Every country develops interpretative rules in accordance with its national culture and traditions, but generally these rules are not articulated and hence it is difficult to identify them and to change them if necessary. It is difficult to understand the rules of one's own country but, even more so, those employed by other national communities. Sometimes insufficient allowance is made for differences, for instance when the Appeasers regarded Hitler as a politician of the same school as themselves, who would rationally accept a chance of satisfying his avowed and fairly legitimate ambitions or when the Czechoslovak leaders were confronted with the cynicism of their Russian counterparts during their enforced negotiations in Moscow in August 1968. It is equally dangerous to proceed on the assumption that the rules which govern the behaviour of others are completely different from one's own, a belief held strongly by some anti-communists.

Interpretation is not fully rational but is often governed by emotions, by the tendency in people to develop 'blind spots' for what is unpleasant, and by wishful thinking. Also the underlying rational processes are unreliable. We can no longer accept the notion of causality as a fully adequate link among events; communist dialectical processes of reasoning lead to interpretations vastly different from those based on western formal logic; the Chinese or the Africans may find both unacceptable.

What we find out about our environment is thus so remote from reality that instead of speaking about knowledge we should employ rather the word 'image'. The important feature of an image is its emphasis on the general outline rather than on detailed items of information. Once a statesman has formed an image of an issue or of another state, this image acts as an organizing device for further information and as a filter through which this information must pass. Images, not detailed information, govern political behaviour. Voters tend to be swayed by the image of the party rather than by specific electoral issues; statesmen deal with another state on the basis of their image of this state rather than on the merits of the concrete problem on hand. The ingrained respective images of a hostile Superpower governed the mutual relations of the Americans and the Russians much more than the details of their actual behaviour. Where this behaviour does not correspond with the image, it is simply ignored—the Russians took no notice of the elementary fact that the allegedly aggressive Americans did not destroy them when they had the monopoly of nuclear weapons, nor did the Americans acknowledge the conciliatory nature of some Soviet moves after Stalin's death.

One of the most significant relationships within the environment is the interaction between domestic and foreign affairs. On the basis of relative security and isolation from foreign affairs, it has been customary for British and American thinkers and statesmen to believe that the two domains are separable and that domestic affairs prevail. Very different is the tradition of the continental countries where such separation has never taken place. Even in powerful states like Napoleonic France of Bismarckian Germany, military requirements and foreign policy objectives invariably mingled with the basic issues of domestic politics. Small and weak states were always even more open to foreign influences. Hence the continental doctrine of *raison d'état* or necessity. Today, even in the West there is no agreement about the interrelation between domestic and foreign affairs—some think that all that states can do is to react to the imperious dictates of foreign policy, especially the implications of the nuclear dilemma; others have retained the idea that statesmen have a freedom of choice, although within the limits environmentally prescribed.

Human minds and energy being limited, excessive concentration on either domestic or foreign affairs must be at the expense of one or the other. Thus during the isolationst era the United States grossly neglected its foreign affairs; perhaps exaggeratedly, George Orwell described in *Nineteen Eighty-Four* what could happen in a 'garrison state' concerned only with its own survival. When popular discontent at home reaches an acute stage, governments often resort to the expedient of diverting attention from domestic to foreign affairs.

Often the domestic–foreign interrelation is blurred. Undoubtedly there was a close connection between Soviet policy in China in the later 'twenties and the dramatic struggle between Stalin and Trotsky at home, or between Soviet action in Hungary in 1956 and the relations between Khrushchev and his opponents. Nevertheless, it is an oversimplification to contend, as is sometimes done, that in both cases domestic considerations fully determined foreign policy, since in both cases the foreign reverses had, in turn, a profound effect on domestic policies. They rendered insecure the incumbents of office and impelled them to stress domestic change in order to divert attention from their failures abroad.

Particularly difficult are the problems of newly-established states where political life at home is generally unsettled and domestic pressures are often insuperable. Violent nationalism, which has brought these states into existence, dictates anti-imperialist and hence generally anti-Western policies, a situation which the communists endeavour to exploit but which is unpalatable to many of the more responsible statesmen.

3
The Foreign Policies of Some Great Powers

Individual Differences and Problems of Comparison

SINCE SOME FACTUAL KNOWLEDGE is essential for the understanding of subsequent generalizations, this chapter discusses the foreign policies of four Powers. It does not aim at giving a full picture; it is much too brief to include more than the barest essentials and, by necessity, it cannot avoid oversimplification.

This book centres around the patterns common to all states, on the interaction of the international system with any of its many units. Needless to say, every single state exhibits also some individual features which defy generalization and call for a detailed study. In order to facilitate comparison it is preferable to use an identical approach to all states studied, to ask always the same questions and to ask them in the same order, even if the relevance of the questions and the nature of the answers are likely to differ. If every state is approached from the angle of its salient characteristics, analysis will be of little use for purposes of comparison. Undoubtedly in time International Relations will evolve a suitable set of questions but none has been generally accepted yet. The scheme here suggested has the advantage of explicitness and systematic arrangement, identical for all case-studies. It coincides sufficiently with many common-sense approaches to be intelligible here but its full justification will become clear only in the light of the following analysis.

The significant factors in the study of foreign policy are arranged in five groups:

1. Capabilities and salient characteristics, such as those deriving from geography or from historical tradition.
2. Peculiarities of the decision-making machinery.
3. Major issues of foreign policy and the means to meet commitments.
4. Attitudes to the most important states and blocs.
5. Attitudes to international order.

The four states discussed are Great Britain, the United States, the Soviet Union, and Communist China. They have been chosen mainly for their individual importance. The two Superpowers are an obvious choice; Britain comes closest to them as a nuclear Power—moreover, she was in the nineteenth century the greatest Power and she is to some extent representative of the colonial Western European states; China is the most populous state on earth and the most important one in Asia; she is the most probable candidate for the status of a Superpower.

The foreign policies of these Powers cannot be considered to be representative of those of other states. On the contrary, they are characterized by an unusual freedom of action based on great capabilities and ambitions; moreover, each of them exhibits strong individual peculiarities. Nevertheless, the parameters of action prescribed by the international environment are similar for all states and within their more limited scope, small Powers can often behave with as great a freedom as their more powerful counterparts. Anyway, even if we choose to regard them as falling within quite a different category, their policies can be subjected to an identical analysis, as their decision-making processes and their interaction with the international environment are not dissimilar.

Great Britain

1. Britain's main historical traditions and social characteristics can be traced to the well-known fact that she is a small crowded island realm situated close to the western shores of Europe. The area, just over 94,000 square miles, is small even by European standards, the population of 55 million[1] ranks equal with the most populous European nations but is extremely small when

[1] All the statistical data are for 1966.

compared with the overseas giants. The Channel, although it
narrows in one place to barely twenty miles, has enabled Britain
to develop both her domestic and her foreign policies on her own
individual lines.

By the end of the Middle Ages Britain had a strong central
government and had made a start with the building of a nation.
Eventually not only the English but also the Welsh and the Scots,
although not the Irish, found accommodation within the broader
scope of the British nation. This 'melting pot' process took place
such a long time ago that the homogeneity of British society was
scarcely endangered by the influx of large numbers of Europeans
and of non-white Commonwealth citizens during and after the
last war. It came however, under a strain in the later sixties, when
Scots and Welsh nationalism raised their heads and the racial
problems arising from the presence of some million non-whites
became acute.

On the background of fair security from foreign invasion and
of growing national integration, Britain evolved a stable political
system, the continuity of which has remained undisturbed ever
since the Glorious Revolution of 1688. The country is not only
homogeneous but also greatly centralized. Most of its social affairs
are conducted by the Government from London, around which
has concentrated nearly one-fifth of its population. The political
parties and pressure-groups, the B.B.C., the most influential
papers, are all national. It is impossible to forecast whether the
Scots and Welsh nationalist movements and the proposals for
regional devolution which became prominent in the later sixties,
will seriously affect centralization.

The effects of Britain's insularity are equally pronounced in
her foreign policy. Although always vitally interested in Europe
and anxious to prevent the danger of its domination by any state
which could menace her security, Britain was no longer part of
Europe ever since her rulers lost Calais, their last continental
possession, in 1558. She became sea-oriented, built the most
powerful navy in the world and the largest colonial empire, and
developed the largest international trade. Her two traditional
concerns were to maintain the balance of power in Europe and to
keep the sea-lanes free, the former by skilful diplomacy and occasional military intervention, the latter through the possession of a
huge navy.

The basis of Britain's power lay in her mature industrial system and in her high standards of living. She has, however, been losing her advantages owing to the more rapid growth of industry in other countries ever since the end of the last century. Since 1945, her economic basis has become increasingly insecure. She has inadequate natural resources and depends on imports of raw materials and food. Her industrial structure requires modernizing, productivity is low, capital investment is insufficient, partly owing to the exceptionally high expenditures on defence and partly to high consumption levels. Britain's economic growth has been slower that that of most other industrialized countries. Her G.N.P. in 1966 was $1,047 billion of which 6·4 per cent was spent on defence, and her per capita income, $1,905, roughly half of that in the United States, is now lower than that in several Western European states.

2. The British machinery for dealing with foreign policy is unique in that it combines a fairly effective ultimate democratic control by the electorate with a freedom of governmental action unparalleled in other democracies. Being centralized and integrated, Britain evolved a political system characterized by two disciplined parties in which no regional or sectional influences can easily interfere with the Government; the intellectual level and the integrity of the Civil Service were exceptional. Since 1945, however, the system has been showing increasing signs of inability to cope with the pressing problems of the day.

This is particularly true about British diplomacy which is probably the most experienced in the world, flexible, pragmatic, and, on the whole, unhindered by wilful interference either of the legislature or of public opinion. It is, however, geared to Britain's traditional position of a World Power which she can no longer afford to maintain while it is insufficiently equipped with the expertise required for the mundane but urgent tasks of promoting British exports.

3. The major problem of contemporary British foreign policy is aptly summed up by Lord Strang, the experienced ex-Permanent Secretary of the Foreign Office:

No British Foreign Secretary ... can get away from the fact that Great Britain is a small, densely populated island with wide overseas interests, inescapably dependent upon foreign trade for the maintenance of its relatively luxurious standard of living.

From the latter part of the last century Britain's supremacy was threatened by Germany which tried to unsettle the balance of power in Europe and then to rival Britain's naval power, while both Germany and the United States were successfully competing with British exports. Thus the major issue of Britain's foreign policy in this century has been how to adapt, to adjust to a world in which British power had shrunk in relation to other states; specifically, to maintain a balance of power in Europe while no longer capable of playing the role of the 'balancer'; to keep the sea-lanes open against more powerful navies; to retain sufficient export markets to pay for the importation of raw materials for industry and of about half of the food consumed; finally, to meet the demands for independence from the far-flung Empire which have become increasingly urgent since the First World War.

Adjustment to the changing conditions of our century was more difficult for Britain than for other countries because she started with world-wide commitments. Up to a point she was highly successful but inevitably difficulties arose, especially since 1945. Today, continuing in the role of a fully armed independent Power requires the costly development of nuclear weapons of dubious and certainly short-lived value; continuing in the role of a world banker and a provider of finance for the Commonwealth, is beyond the economic capacity of the country. Although Britain cut down her commitments rapidly, and on the whole successfully, particularly in emancipating her dependencies, the lingering burdens crippled her economy. Moreover, she committed some errors, the most serious of which were the ill-fated Suez expedition in 1956 and the long neglect of European integration.

4. Britain's most intimate foreign relations are with the Commonwealth countries, with the United States, and with western Europe. After the successful rebellion of the Thirteen Colonies she was not tardy in preventing similar occurrences elsewhere in the Empire. By an unexampled process of peaceful emancipation she granted independence first to the colonies of settlement with a predominantly white population, then also to other colonies. In

the brief period since 1945 she emancipated over 600 million people, and was left in 1962 with only 35 million, some of whom were scheduled for early independence. On the whole, although a residue of anti-imperialist sentiment lingers, relations with the emancipated dependencies developed in a friendly way and were institutionalized in the loose informal framework of the Commonwealth.

In the post-war period, the attractions of the Commonwealth idea were great. It seemed to offer political opportunities for perpetuating British world influence based upon voluntary co-operation instead of imperial rule; economic opportunities for developing the important existing markets under the protection of the imperial preferences; moral leadership opportunities for establishing a unique pattern of racial co-operation. Unfortunately, the Commonwealth proved disappointing on all three scores. Politically, the new members were too attached to independence and to nonalignment to cultivate an attachment to Britain, while her diminished power status decreased her influence upon the ex-Dominions, too. The widespread desire for economic independence and the diminishing importance of the British market combined in frustrating economic expectations. The multi-racial idea was hampered by the white supremacy in Southern Africa. While South Africa was forced to resign in 1961, the Commonwealth faced a severe crisis over the indecisive British reaction to the Unilateral Declaration of Independence by Rhodesia in 1963. This crisis is still unresolved. Few would quarrel with the opinion that by the mid-sixties, the Commonwealth has ceased to be regarded as a sphere of British foreign policy equivalent in importance to Western Europe or to the North Atlantic.

British relations with the United States are based on racial and cultural affinities with the original settlers. Largely owing to the feeling that the Americans were less dangerous than other nations because they were of British origin and were interested mainly in their own remote hemisphere, despite the brief clash in 1812 and several acute crises, by the end of the last century relations between the two countries reached a stage in which an armed conflict became unthinkable. Britain readily accepted the growing American power—she supported the Monroe Doctrine, she gave in on the boundary disputes, early in the twentieth century she abandoned her share in the Isthmus Canal and withdrew her Navy from the Caribbean, in 1922 she conceded to the United States naval parity. Both countries fought together in the latter stages of the two World Wars, and Britain joined security arrangements, particularly NATO, within which the United States is undisputedly the senior partner.

The transition was smooth but not entirely without friction. Britain endeavoured to accept her loss of power and the role of a junior partner on the level of 'special relations' with the United States based historically on their partnership in the Second World War and prolonged by the fact that Britain became an independent nuclear Power.

Gradually, however, her junior role became increasingly obvious and the relationship with the United States less 'special'. The watershed was the Suez Crisis in 1956 which fully showed that, in any major foreign policy move, Britain had become dependent upon United States support. The breach was soon healed but the degree of dependence increased, especially in the sixties, when Britain became dependent on the United States for the supply of the Polaris missile, the present mainstay of her strategic nuclear force. While for Britain the relationship with the United States is of primary, vital importance, for the United States it is not.

At first Britain remained aloof from the post-war European integration moves and refused to join the European communities when they were formed, giving priority to other spheres. Owing to the rapid economic and political successes of the E.E.C. together with her disappointment over the rate of her own economic growth and over the evolution of the Commonwealth, and consistently prodded to do so by the United States, Britain eventually applied for membership of the E.E.C. in August 1961. This step was justly regarded as a watershed in British history; it expressed Britain's realization that she could not maintain her traditional position as one of the few Great Powers, that her capabilities were insufficient to match those of the Superpowers. The French, jealous to preserve an undisputed leadership of the European Communities, opposed British entry then, and again, in 1967–8, when from a position of increased economic weakness, Britain renewed her application. Despite these setbacks, Britain's preference for Western Europe as the major sphere of her foreign policy, has become firmly established. It is now the official policy of all the major political parties, it commands the majority support of public opinion, it has been manifested and reinforced by the decision to withdraw the military forces from East of Suez, it has been apparently accepted as final by the members of the Commonwealth.

As regards her relations with the Communist bloc, Britain was the main opponent to communist expansion for some eighteen months after the termination of the war, until she was replaced in this task by the United States. Later, however, her attitudes to the Soviet Union and particularly to Communist China became more conciliatory than those of the United States. She has, however, been unsuccessful in her sporadic attempts to play the role of an intermediary between the United States and the Communist Powers.

5. Throughout modern times Britain has been closely identified with international order: she was one of the main participants in the European balance of power system; she took a leading part in the evolution of the norms of international law; she upheld the principles of the freedom of the seas and of international trade; against the background of her security and of the resulting 'moral opportunity', her statesmen were able to observe moral rules to a greater extent than most other statesmen. Having helped to shape the order and to formulate its norms largely according to her views and interests, and having secured an enormous empire and great wealth, Britain naturally became a staunch upholder of the *status quo*.

From 1919 onwards it was fairly obvious that the balance of power system could not be revived in its nineteenth-century form and that Britain was no longer sufficiently powerful to act as a 'balancer'. Nevertheless, possibly this attachment to the international order which had been so advantageous for Britain in the past, was the major obstacle to her full-hearted acceptance of the new ideas of collective security embodied in international organization. Britain was unwilling to pay the lion's share in its maintenance under the League of Nations but was likewise lukewarm in supporting it under the United Nations when her share became very much smaller. She remains a loyal but unenthusiastic member, despite the fact that the United Nations strongly

condemned the Suez intervention in 1956 and, often irrespon-
sibly, has interfered in colonial administration.

The main problem which remains open is whether Britain
should continue more or less on the present lines or whether she
should gradually give up her individual contribution to international order and merge with other Western European states.
Here, as in her attitude to collective security, she is faced not only
with the unpleasant prospect of curtailing her sovereignty but
also of having to accept in advance, against her tradition of
pragmatism, a fixed constitutional design. Moreover, although
the other members of the Western European Communities support her entry, she is still blocked by the French veto.

The United States

1. American politics differ from British politics in scale—the
United States has a territory of over three million square miles
and in the sixties its population reached 200 million. In so far as
they reflect isolation from Europe, American traditions resemble
those of the British. Protected by the whole width of the Atlantic
which was under the control of the benevolent British Navy,
throughout the nineteenth century the Americans practised
'splendid isolation' and concentrated upon their continent. They
conquered and colonized a large part of it, pushing forward 'the
frontier of civilization', and they evoked the 'Monroe Doctrine'
which aimed at the exclusion of rivals from the remainder. They
rapidly developed the great natural riches of their country and
built up an industry on a scale hitherto unequalled.

The Americans had only one outside interest—to avoid an
imperious incursion from Europe. Here they relied upon Britain
to maintain the balance of power and to prevent the rise of a
dangerous imperialist state. Consequently they had scarcely any
foreign policy at all and their traditions in this field are extremely new. This preoccupation with domestic and continental
affairs engendered the American conviction that the domestic
and foreign spheres could be permanently separated, and also
what some writers call 'the myth of omnipotence'—the belief that
the unparalleled American domestic successes could be repeated
also in international relations.

At the turn of the century the United States embarked on a

policy of territorial expansion in the Pacific and the Far East. Its aims were not very clear—by and large they were to keep China independent—as a counterbalance to the rising might of Japan, and open—as a market for American trade.

The great open spaces of North America were almost empty and required labour for their development. First slaves were imported from Africa; their emancipated descendants amount to over 10 per cent of the American population today and, owing to the racial difference, have not been effectively assimilated. Then millions of European immigrants of various nationalities flocked into the United States. Thus, in complete contrast to homogeneous Britain, American society incorporated many different elements in quite recent times. The original common mould was largely shaped by British traditions, but the vast spaces, the persistence of the individual identities of the separate colonies, and 'the melting pot' of the various national and racial strains, produced a highly decentralized system characterized by a federal constitution, by lack of discipline within the two great national political parties, and by the prevalence of regional and particularist interests. It is not only political power that is decentralized; there are also no national mass media, excepting the occasional national hook-ups of television networks. In the sixties, the political system entered a period of crisis. The racial problems became increasingly acute and public opinion split over the American involvement in Vietnam; urban violence increased, culminating in recurrent summer riots and in the assassinations of one President and one Presidential candidate.

The basis of United States power lies in her great natural resources, in her industrial system which, by any criteria, is the most evolved in the world, in her lead in technological advance, and in her unparalleled standards of living. In 1966, her population was 197 million, her G.N.P. was $743 billion, of which 9.2 per cent was spent on defence: the per capita income amounted to $3,776.

2. The nature of American democracy, particularly decentralization, the division of constitutional powers, and the impact of public opinion, are gravely prejudicial to an efficient foreign policy. De Tocqueville's famous remarks made over a century ago are still fully pertinent:

Foreign politics demand scarcely any of these qualities which are peculiar to democracy; they require, on the contrary, the perfect use of almost all those in which it is deficient . . . a democracy can only with great difficulties regulate the details of an important undertaking, persevere in a fixed design, and work out its execution in spite of serious obstacles. It cannot combine its measures with secrecy or await their consequences with patience.

American governmental machinery is extremely cumbersome. The President is undoubtedly the chief decision-maker within the Executive, but under him some 45 or more agencies deal with foreign affairs. The Congress which, on the basis of the 'checks and balances' doctrine, has co-ordinate powers, interferes; and, in the absence of party discipline, the President cannot control the regional and the sectional interests within it. Moreover, as national congressional elections take place every two years, the opinions of the electorate at large incessantly intrude.

Until 1945 American diplomacy was relatively undeveloped and suffered from inadequate apparatus and insufficient professionalism; it was ill-equipped to cope with the difficult post-war tasks. Since then the Americans have built up the largest diplomatic service on earth with missions in nearly all other states. This service lacks long tradition and is gravely handicapped by the activities of poorly co-ordinated intelligence and, to a lesser extent, also aid-giving agencies, as well as by the constant intrusion of domestic policies. Its shortcomings and occasional blunders must be viewed against the background of a generally successful development.

3. Within the first half of this century the Americans, who formerly had little or no foreign policy, suddenly became one of the two Superpowers, and their world-wide commitments required from them a complete mental reorientation. In spite of occasional disturbance, on the whole they were successful in their adjustments. When their security was menaced by the prospects of a German victory, they reluctantly took part in the First World War; equally unwillingly they entered the Second World War in 1941; but in both wars they fought with will and determination. When Britain was unable to continue her task of containing Communism, the United States stepped in in March 1947, with the 'Truman Doctrine', and became the protagonist in the 'cold

war'. With the Marshall Plan and NATO she stabilized the situation in Europe, but her interventions in Asia were less successful.

Undoubtedly the major issues of American foreign policy today, military, political, economic, and ideological, all stem from her position as a Superpower balancing the power of the Soviet Union. American foreign policy requires great expenditure of money, constant vigilance, and alert diplomacy. The Americans have scored successes but have also suffered defeats, and the clashing demands of their world-wide commitments often confront them with apparently insoluble dilemmas. United States expenditure on defence and for other purposes of foreign policy has been steadily mounting, especially the cost of the intervention in Vietnam, but its economy can sustain it.

In the order of their historical evolution, the major direct American foreign policy interest lies in the Western Hemisphere; the somewhat less direct interest in Europe is of equal age, whereas interest in Asia stems from the end of the last century only. The direct interest in the Western Hemisphere persists but, with the rapid growth in the population centres on the Pacific seaboard, Asia and the Pacific have become a close rival to Europe and the North Atlantic.

4. Ever since her rise to the position of a Superpower, the United States foreign relations with the Soviet Union, her fellow Superpower, have become outstandingly important, including, as they do, the element of nuclear rivalry. In the 'cold war', the main objective of the United States was to deter a direct nuclear attack on the territory of the United States or of American allies, and to contain communist expansion, the danger of which has gradually spread from Europe and the Far East to all other continents and regions. In spite of the loose proclamation of a more active policy of 'liberation' in 1952, the American attitude to the Soviet Union remained fundamentally passive, as expressed in the formula of 'containment', coined by the influential diplomat, George F. Kennan. The United States pursued this policy by accumulating massive armaments, by concluding a series of alliances, and by establishing foreign bases. It furnished lavish aid, military and economic, to its allies and also to neutrals. The Communists scored a victory in China in 1949 but elsewhere the Americans

succeeded in containing them—in Korea through a full-scale war fought with conventional weapons. Only in Vietnam have they been unsuccessful, despite their large-scale involvement.

Stalin's death in 1953 ended the era of crude Soviet military menace. Thereafter the conflict began to shift to economic and ideological competition to win the sympathy of the uncommitted, neutral states in Asia and in Africa. Gradually the two Superpowers began to find accommodation on several important issues, including those of nuclear strategy and of their respective spheres of interest. After having been brought to the brink of a direct clash during the Cuban Missile Crisis in October 1963, the 'cold war' gradually changed into what the Americans usually call a '*détente*' and the Russians 'peaceful co-existence'. Tensions continue and it is difficult to decide which side is more obstructive in changing the nature of the relationship or to estimate how deleterious will be the effect of the massive Soviet military intervention in Czechoslovakia in August 1968.

American relations with China did not, however, improve. After a direct armed clash in Korea, the Americans remained entrenched in their bases on Okinawa and on Taiwan, and became gradually involved in a massive military intervention in support of the anti-communist regime in South Vietnam. Chinese success in developing nuclear weapons exacerbated the antagonism. Undoubtedly the Sino-Soviet rift which came out into the open by the end of the fifties and became acute by the mid sixties has contributed to the United States–Soviet '*détente*' but it has also introduced an additional element of uncertainty into their relationship.

American relations with other regions and states were to a very large extent a reflection of their relations with the Communist Powers; sometimes, to the detriment of American interests, they were governed rather by the dictates of the 'cold war' than by considerations arising directly from their relations with these other states. This applied even to allies: in the Western Hemisphere the Americans were unavailingly trying to transform the Organization of American States into an effective anti-communist alliance, but, since 1961, they were compelled to endure the pro-communist Government of Fidel Castro in Cuba; in the later fifties, their most successful coalition, the North Atlantic Treaty Organization lost much of its urgency of purpose and proved incapable of resolving several serious problems of co-operation.

Within the Afro-Asian realm, United States interest in Asia is much the stronger one as here it is involved in a policy of 'containment' of Communist China. Although China is lacking in the capabilities for large-scale expansion and may not have any intention of it, the United States has become involved in supporting anti-communist regimes in the region which has led to their intervention in Vietnam. This intervention has further added to the stigma of colonialism affecting the Americans owing to their links with the major colonial Powers and to their stress upon alliances and military methods. Nor are they capable of finding a suitable foil to the communist formula for rapid economic growth; their fairly lavishly distributed economic aid is governed mainly by political considerations and it fails to secure either economic growth, or lasting friendship, or even benevolent neutrality.

5. Through traditions held in common with Britain, the Americans felt identified with the international order of the nineteenth century more than any other non-European state. They contributed to the evolution of some international norms, especially to the law of neutrality; throughout their period of isolationism they remained intensely interested in the maintenance of the balance of power in Europe even though they did not play an active part in it. When the balance was seriously threatened by the Germans in the two wars and by the Russians since, they soon stepped into the breach.

While the British attitude to a new international order embodied in international institutions was consistent, the American attitude was not. The League of Nations was Wilson's brainchild, but the Senate refused to ratify the Peace Treaty of Versailles and to join the Organization. During the Second World War the Americans were responsible for the setting up of the United Nations, but this time they continued to play a central part in its operation. At first they were able to use the organization to their national advantage since, with the support of the Latin American states (20 out of the original membership of 50) and of their Western European allies, they commanded crushing anti-Russian majorities on all important matters which came up before the General Assembly. They greatly benefited from the

United Nations sponsorship of what was in fact an American action in Korea. But, even in the sixties, after the easy majorities disappeared in a membership which had more than doubled, the Americans retained a more positive attitude to the Organization than any other Great Power and remained the most generous contributor to its finance. Being located in New York and thus providing local news, the United Nations figured in the American press much more frequently than in the press of any other country.

It may be added that the United States—in concert with the Soviet Union—could introduce a world-order based on the drawing of boundaries between the spheres of interests of the two Superpowers. Such an order is unlikely. The Communist world is split; communist expansion into the Western Hemisphere militates against such accommodation; moreover, the Americans feel a fundamental antagonism to Communism and could not accept communist rule over a third of mankind even as a factor of stability.

The Soviet Union

1. Any analysis of Soviet affairs must inevitably include a discussion of communist ideology. All countries are governed by systems of values and beliefs which we now call ideologies, but whereas in Britain or the United States or any other established non-communist country, ideologies have organically developed together with other political and social traditions, in the Soviet Union the communist ideology was imposed upon the country in 1917 and its exact relation to the tsarist heritage is still disputed.

Although most Marxists emphatically deny that the geographical position of a country may have a determining effect on its foreign policy, this is more clearly the case with Russia than with many other countries. Russia is the very antithesis of Britain both in size and location: it is by far the largest state on earth, embracing over $8\frac{1}{2}$ million square miles, fully one-half of the Eurasian continent. No 'natural frontiers' exist to which Russia could aspire since no physical features delimit the central Russian plain. The country is clearly indefensible, and the fluctuating nature of Russian frontiers reflects the strength or weakness of the central government. For three centuries Russia was under the

Tartar yoke and as late as in the seventeenth century she had temporarily a Polish ruler.

While the indeterminate nature of Russian frontiers made the country an easy prey for attacks, it also encouraged the Russians to seek security through expansion. They expanded in all directions, reaching the physical limits of the Arctic and Pacific Oceans and clashing with neighbouring countries everywhere else. In contrast to the relative isolation of Britain and the United States, Russia was in constant interaction with her neighbours—when she was weak and disunited she was subject to depradations, when she was strong and united she expanded as far as possible. The traditional aims of Russian foreign policy are to absorb or truncate weak neighbours and to exercise as much control as possible over those unwilling to yield and able to resist. Her specific territorial objectives are sea-outlets, ice-free ports, the subject of the historical drives towards the Straits, towards the Persian Gulf, and towards the Yellow Sea.

The imperious demands of foreign policy set such a premium upon unity and centralization that Russia achieved a fair degree of both despite her enormous area and her large population divided into some 150 ethnic and linguistic groups which differ greatly in many important characteristics. Although her constitution is federal in form, the Soviet Union perpetuates the tsarist tradition of central control which is now exercised by the Communist Party.

The October Revolution in 1917 brought into power the bolsheviks whose Marxist ideology not only prescribed a new leading objective of world revolution but also a new system of knowledge and new strategies of foreign policy. During the twenties the break with the past seemed complete: the Soviet rulers were pursuing their goal of world revolution in a ruthless and unprecedented fashion. When, however, in the late twenties this goal was replaced by that of 'building socialism in one country', and when various traditional Russian policies and ways of behaviour were revived, the question of the inter-relation between ideology and national tradition began to loom large. While some western experts contend that Soviet foreign policy is still rigidly controlled by ideology, others claim that this is merely a thin disguise for traditional tsarist policies which are no more than the obvious reaction to the challenges arising in Russia's environment. Others again try to combine both approaches and study the changes in ideology in actual Soviet practice.

The Soviet regime successfully controlled the country, industrialized it, won the Second World War and recovered from its colossal destruction, but only through the exercise of a strict and ruthless totalitarian regime, oppressive to the citizens. By the end of the Second World War, the Union secured the position of a Superpower but, from the death of Stalin in 1953 onward, she has been facing increasingly insistent demands for liberalization of the regime and for an increased supply of consumer goods.

The Soviet Union possesses tremendous natural resources, but an unevenly developed industrial system. Although her rockets and some of her heavy machinery surpass in their sophistication those manufactured in the United States, she is quite backward in most branches of consumer goods and she cannot master the organization of agriculture in which collective and state farms have proved quite inadequate. In 1966 the Soviet population was 233 million; her G.N.P. was estimated to be $335 billion, of which 8·9 per cent were spent on defence. Her per capita income at $1,437 was rather low, when compared with that of the United States.[1]

2. The making of foreign policy in the Soviet Union as in all single-party authoritarian states is characterized by complete Party control. The governmental apparatus, including the Foreign Ministry, are mere executants of the policies decided by it. Within the Party, power was formerly rigidly concentrated in the hands of Stalin, but under the 'collective leadership' which succeeded him it was vested in the Praesidium or Politburo which now numbers eleven. Between 1956 and 1963 the First Secretary of the Party, Mr. Khrushchev, had dominated Soviet politics and was internationally the only prominent figure, but he was not a dictator with unlimited powers; he depended upon the other members of the Praesidium, and also, to a much smaller extent, on the members of the larger Central Committee of the Party. Since the removal of Khrushchev no individual became predominant in Soviet leadership.

[1] Soviet statistics are not fully comparable with Western statistics and the data are unreliable. Chinese figures are even less reliable—they amount to mere informed guesses.

Soviet diplomacy is unorthodox; it engages in wide-spread espionage and propaganda and is therefore generally distrusted. Moreover, it is rigid and is slavishly dependent on central orders. Consequently, in spite of the large funds at its disposal and the great pool of ability from which it can draw, it is not particularly successful. There are no signs that the position has changed since Stalin's death; the blundering treatment of the Czechoslovak crisis in 1968, indicates that it is essentially similar.

3. Soviet foreign policy can be judged in different ways because we cannot be certain to which of their objectives the Russians give priority; in fact the Russian leaders themselves are divided, or unclear, or both. The Soviet Union is a rapidly developing country in which the standard of living of the citizens is still very low. Although it is working at full strength and rapidly expanding, the Soviet economy still cannot provide enough for the growing needs of consumption, the mounting military expenditure, and foreign aid. In the sixties it became obvious that, although in possession of all the elements of power, the Soviet Union was feeling the strain rather acutely.

It is not a case of the proverbial choice between guns and butter; all Soviet rulers chose and are likely to go on choosing guns as long as they deem these essential for national security. The question now is to what extent they feel that they must continuously work with all the means at their disposal for a world revolution which, according to the Marxist doctrine, is anyway inevitable. Even if this goal retains its high value, they have now much more efficient means to increase their power through further economic development at home than through political and military expansion. Moreover, having already secured a fairly high level of industrial and social advancement, they are likely to be chary of risking their achievements through foreign adventures, and this advancement may have to some extent transformed their ideology. Finally, although at the moment this is highly speculative, in view of the difficulties arising from their relations with Communist China, the Russians may find the prospect of an all-communist world much less attractive; ultimately they may find solidarity with the highly industrialized countries of the West and with the white race.

These are, of course, western interpretations of the major issues

of Soviet foreign policy. It is quite likely that many, perhaps most
of the Soviet leaders genuinely believe their own protestations
that Soviet foreign policy is defensive, that the Soviet Union is
threatened from all directions by the United States which has
established a ring of alliances and military bases all around the
Union, and which conducts a strongly anti-communist policy.
The future development of Soviet foreign policy is bound to
revolve around these two fundamental issues; priority of domestic
or foreign commitments, and evaluation of American intentions.

4. Thus, clearly Soviet relations with the United States dominate
the whole of Soviet foreign policy. It is difficult to appreciate from
the outside what the Russians exactly mean by their slogan of
'peaceful co-existence' with the capitalist world. Although crude
military expansionism ceased with Stalin's death, a fundamental
hostility and distrust persists. The Chinese Communists and, in
all probability, also many Soviet Communists still think in terms
of the ultimately inevitable was between the United States and
the Soviet Union. Even Mr. Khrushchev, the main architect of
peaceful co-existence, repeatedly made it clear that it meant to
him not the abandonment of hostility but merely a shift of the
conflict from the military to other fields. To some extent Soviet-
American relations are bound to depend on what the Americans
do and on how they behave but, in all likelihood, they depend
very much more on the evolution of Soviet society and of communist ideology.

Soviet relations with other communist states give rise to problems which are much more complicated and independent of the
cold war than similar problems confronting the United States in
relations with its allies. Until 1945 these countries were neither
Communist nor under Russian rule. In conformity both with
tsarist tradition and with the goal of a world revolution, the
Soviet Union imposed communist regimes wherever the Red
Army marched: local communists seized power by themselves
only in Yugoslavia and later also in China. It was difficult for the
Soviet Union to control the new communist governments as they
habitually do communist parties abroad. Already in 1947–8 they
tried in vain to squash nationalist opposition in Yugoslavia; in
1956 Poland and Hungary asserted their individualities.

Of greatest importance was the Sino-Soviet rift which came out into the open in the late fifties and gradually grew until China clearly became a dangerous opponent of the Soviet Union, threatening her long, 4,300 miles frontier by her claims for the return of lost territories, rivalling her as a more radical leader of international communism, admittedly with only limited success. In the late sixties, the communist bloc further loosened, with Albania coming out firmly on the side of China, with Rumania asserting herself through an independent foreign policy, and, in 1968, through Czechoslovakia rapidly liberalizing her regime. With the assistance of similarly apprehensive regimes in Eastern Germany, Poland, Hungary, and Bulgaria, the Russians first threatened the liberalizers and then had to resort to a large-scale military occupation of Czechoslovakia, showing how brittle the solidarity of the bloc had become. Patriotism united the Czechs and the Slovaks against the occupiers. Instead of being monolithic the communist bloc is now clearly polycentric; the various governments are dependent on the Soviet Union militarily and economically and cannot effectively defend themselves. Nevertheless, they are able to exercise a fair degree of independence, according to their individual strength and determination.

In their relations with the non-committed countries, the Soviet leaders came up against a contradiction between their support for world revolution and for foreign communists and their interest in alignment with 'bourgeois-nationalist' governments which are willing to stay out of American alliances. They were inconsistent and vacillating. After initial opposition to the new governments, they unsuccessfully attempted to cajole them into an anti-western 'camp of peace' which would embrace the communist and the non-committed blocs. In the early sixties they abandoned this policy as unpromising.

At first, the Russians scored diplomatic successes in Asia, Africa, and Latin America owing to two important assets which are effective in spite of their contradictory diplomacy: the imperialist taint of the Western Powers and the prestige of the communist formula for 'pulling oneself up by one's own boot straps', of economic growth through central planning. By and large, the Western imperialist excesses and exploitation are now a matter of the past, and Russian economic growth cannot be repeated elsewhere in more difficult conditions with the same degree of success. Moreover, the Russians are suffering from the competition of the Chinese and cannot afford to provide substantial economic aid except to a few selected countries.

5. In many respects the Soviet rulers have reverted to tsarist traditions, but it was obviously impossible for them to build upon the traditional Russian attitudes to international order. The tsarist regime participated as one of the major Powers in the Concert of Europe and even wished to transform it into a kind of world government which would intervene whenever necessary to preserve the *status quo*. The communist regime pursued a policy which is the very opposite of this: instead of being wholeheartedly conservative, it was revolutionary; instead of wishing to preserve the existing order, it aimed at its complete overthrow. As long as the final goal of world revolution persists, the Soviet rulers cannot take part in international transactions on the same footing as other, non-revolutionary states. They reject the existing order as undesirable and untenable, even if possibly they no longer consider the task of abolishing it as very urgent. 'Peaceful co-existence' with non-communist states is merely tactics, though probably quite long-range tactics.

Soviet attitudes to the institutions serving international order shape accordingly. The Russian leaders believe in one type of internationalism alone—the proletarian one, through the solidarity of the working classes with the communist governments. Their relations with non-communist governments are fundamentally inimical if not actively hostile. Their diplomacy is less a way of arriving at an agreement with other states than a method of conducting hostile propaganda. To them, international law which expresses and buttresses the existing order is as undesirable as the order itself; international institutions are controlled by and serve the ends of capitalist states.

All these declared attitudes and intentions certainly do not represent a faithful picture of Soviet diplomatic practice which frequently deviates from them and increasingly resembles the orthodox diplomacy of Western Powers. Thus, when interested in the conclusion of a specific treaty, the Russians stress their habit of faithful adherence to agreements: in the mid-thirties, when afraid of Hitler, they tried to bring to life the moribund collective security system of the League; in 1950, when confronted with the United Nations support for the American action in South

Korea, they immediately resumed participation in the organs of the institution which they had been boycotting for several months; they began to represent themselves as defenders of the non-committed countries against imperialism and cashed in on their anti-colonial and hence anti-Western sentiments to harass the Western Powers in the General Assembly. At the same time, wishing to avoid the possibility of an independent, i.e. potentially anti-communist activity of the Organization, they tried to induce the neutrals to support the Soviet proposals for the splitting of the central position of the Secretary-General into a 'troika', a three-man directorate, one of whom would represent the uncommitted states.

Until Stalin's death the fundamental hostility of the Soviet Union to the existing international order could not be doubted, but one cannot reject the possibility that the Soviet Union has now shed her aggressively revolutionary character and is becoming more conservative, more ready to participate in the preservation of the existing order within which she has secured herself a leading position. She has to compete with the more radical Communist China and has much to lose in a general war.

Communist China

1. The Chinese variant of Communism is much more extreme and virulent than the Russian, partly because China's problems are more acute and her demands less satisfied, and partly because she is still in her early post-revolutionary stage—the Chinese revolution was completed only in 1949, thirty-two years after the October Revolution in Russia. Nevertheless, since Russia and not China is the main champion of world revolution, and since the main Chinese ambitions are limited to Asia and coterminous with the traditional sphere of interest and influence of the Chinese Empire, there is no dispute about the significance of China's national traditions, which go back some 5,000 years.

Like Russia, China is predominantly a land Power. Although she commands a long sea-coast, only during the period of the early Mings, about the time of the Tudors, did the Chinese develop a powerful ocean-going navy. In Chinese history the pendulum swings from integration into a loose imperial whole, to disintegration into many provinces governed by warlords; recurrent barbarian invasions from Central Asia are followed by the absorption and assimilation of the invaders; dynasties follow one another—according to Chinese political theory each receives a mandate from heaven and retains it so long as it can cope with the tasks of government but loses it if it fails. The communist government can be understood as another dynastic government replacing its predecessor which lost its mandate from heaven, but a government with a difference. It has introduced European technology and communist political and industrial techniques into a hitherto oriental background.

China with her more than $4\frac{1}{2}$ million square miles ranks among the largest states on earth although she is much smaller than the Soviet Union. Nevertheless her population, by far the largest of any single state, uncomfortably crowds the area. According to Chinese statistics in 1957 the population was 646,530,000; in 1966 the figure probably surpassed 700 million. Food-production in China depends upon colossal irrigation works for which the central government has always been responsible, and the totalitarian communist society perpetuates and develops the tradition of the 'hydraulic' society of China.

Tremendous distances and poor communication obstructed full political integration, which the Chinese achieved only a few times and for brief periods. Nevertheless, they developed a strong cultural unity and managed to assimilate the invading barbarians and some non-Chinese border-people. They gradually spread their influence in the neighbouring countries; the 'Kingdom of the Middle' became the centre of a vast political system with vassals and satellites and tribute-payers in various degrees of dependence. Throughout history Chinese borders have violently fluctuated and shifted, so that modern China can claim territories which had once been Chinese from every single one of her neighbours.

During its short period in power, the Communist regime has mobilized the population politically and economically in an unprecedented fashion but only at the cost of increasingly grave crises. The last one of these, the 'Cultural Revolution', which began in 1966, led to prolonged factional fighting which paralysed China's educational system and gravely disturbed her industrial production. Early in 1969, its conclusion was not yet in sight.

The economic basis of China's power is uncertain. The country is likely to command considerable mineral resources but not many of them have been explored and even fewer are being fully exploited. China's industrial development started on a large scale only under the Communist regime, but was disrupted when Soviet aid was stopped. It lags far behind that of the Soviet Union. The Chinese have managed to develop thermo-nuclear technology and some heavy industry but these are uncharacteristic; China remains a predominantly peasant society. In 1966 her G.N.P. was estimated to be in the neighbourhood of $80 billion of which some 10 per cent were spent on defence, and her per capita income was no more than some $85.

2. The institutions of Communist China have been moulded on those of the Soviet Union, but China, being nationally nearly homogeneous, did not employ the federal form. As in the Soviet Union, the Communist Party is supreme, but it had a somewhat different history: it never went through a period of one-person dictatorship as monolithic as that of Stalin. Scarcely a decade after the final success of the Revolution, the Chinese Party leadership split on lines very similar to those observable in the Soviet Union, though in China the radical wing is more powerful and controls policy. The split became increasingly acute, eventually leading to a sustained but so far unsuccessful attempt by Chairman Mao to reimpose his control through the 'Cultural Revolution'.

3. Compared with the Soviet Union, China has little reason to be satisfied with the *status quo*. The Chinese are poverty-stricken, and despite their enormous efforts under communist leadership they have made little progress towards industrialization. Moreover, they advance several territorial claims based upon national security and upon historical rights—notably their claim for the incorporation of Taiwan, at present under the control of the rival Nationalist Government, which enjoys the support of the United States.

Relief of poverty is undoubtedly the most urgent of governmental tasks, and the Chinese are under much greater pressure than the Russians to give priority to requirements of economic growth over those of foreign policy. Perhaps in the long run these pressures must prevail, but so far the Chinese leaders have given little indication that they acknowledge such priority. Their foreign relations with the United States, with the Soviet Union, and with their neighbours seem to be determined chiefly by political considerations without much regard for securing foreign aid. Again we must allow for the possibility that, whereas to western observers, the Chinese leaders seem to be governed by the wrong priorities, to themselves their foreign policies may appear to be dictated by national security and national dignity. They are probably genuinely apprehensive of an American-supported invasion from Taiwan which would find some following among the population of the mainland. In all likelihood, the historical record of Russian encroachments upon Chinese territory makes them anxious to guard against the continuation of the process, and to reverse it, if possible. Everywhere else, too, they aspire to the old imperial frontiers and to the establishment of control over neighbouring states through communist governments dependent on China.

4. The tradition of being self-centred and the absence of adequate capabilities for a world role, combine to restrict China to a more pronouncedly regional sphere of operations than those of the previously discussed Powers. Her antagonism to the United States is based fundamentally on Asian politics. The Chinese cannot forget the United States support for the Nationalists during the Civil War and now on Taiwan, the interventions in Korea and in Vietnam, close to the Chinese borders. The conflict includes an ideological element and is usually presented by the Chinese in an ideological garb but it can be equally well interpreted as one of purely political power.

The basic importance of China's relations with the Soviet Union is even greater as they share a land-frontier 4,300 miles long. Despite the common communist ideology and the common hostility to the United States, this relationship has been far from easy. The Russians only reluctantly restored to China her Manchurian concessions and gave her inadequate economic aid. An open rift arose in the later fifties and became exacerbated since. The Chinese are unwilling to conform to the Soviet Union in their domestic or in their foreign policies. As the Russians withdrew aid facilities and refused to assist China in her nuclear programme, the Chinese became increasingly hostile, competing with the Russians for the leadership of world communism and raising claims for the restoration of the territories forfeited to Russia in the nineteenth century. In 1969 armed clashes occurred on the disputed boundaries.

With her Asian neighbours and near-neighbours which once came within the orbit of the peripheries of her ancient empire, China occasionally revives her shadowy claims giving rise to a suspicion of an expansionist policy. These Asian countries are the major sphere of her operations also in her two attempts to play a world role—either as a leader of an anti-imperialist bloc or as a leader of the international communist movement. In both guises China acted in opposition to the Soviet Union—first in endeavouring to befriend the anti-imperialist but non-communist states, which culminated in the Bandung Conference in April 1955, while the Russians persisted in a rigid 'two-camps' doctrine; then in trying to obtain influence over the international communist movement.

Chinese forays outside Asia proved futile. Her influence over Albania, which is of marginal importance, persists, but her intercessions on behalf of Eastern European states in 1956 and in 1968 were ineffective and her influence in Cuba and in a few African states, only ephemeral. 1965 was a very bad year for Chinese world ambitions—it was marked by her defeat on the issue of Soviet participation at the Second Bandung Conference in Algiers which, anyway, proved abortive, by the failure of various Chinese-inspired liberation-movements in Africa and in Latin America, by the liquidation of the friendly Indonesian Communist Party and the severance of the Peking–Djakarta axis, and by a firm United States involvement in the Vietnam conflict. This was followed by the 'Cultural Revolution' with its debilitating effects. China's nuclear weapons development, although successful, scarcely made up for these.

China proved powerful on the battlefield when she held the United States to a stalemate in the Korean War in 1951 and when she scored victories against India in 1962. She has by far the largest land-army on earth adequate to overwhelm any of her neighbours except the Soviet Union and perhaps India, but it is short of modern equipment and of logistic support. Moreover, China is highly deficient in capital and other resources for industrialization, and she clearly depends on the extensive support of at least one of the two Superpowers. She is now seriously weakened by the prolonged 'Cultural Revolution'.

5. Logically, China's attitude to international order is more negative than Russia's. Her historical traditions are purely oriental and she tends to revert to the disdainful style of imperial diplomacy in which all other states were treated as barbarian and subordinate. Her aims are pronouncedly revisionist and, unlike the Soviet Union, she has not had much opportunity or reason to demonstrate even a temporary and limited acceptance of international law or to join international institutions. China is a founder-member of the United Nations and one of the five Permanent Members of the Security Council, but she is still represented by the Nationalist Government of China whose rule is limited to Taiwan. As a result of American pressures, the Communist Government was not only deprived of representation in the United Nations but was also branded by it as an aggressor in Korea and was subjected to United Nations sanctions.

China's pronouncedly negative attitude to international order may ultimately wreck the possibility of new arrangements. The Chinese Government is in no way subservient to the Soviet Government, and even if the Russians genuinely wish to accept some scheme of disarmament, agreement could easily founder on the lack of Chinese consent.

4

Interaction among States and State Power

Conflict, Competition, and Co-operation

RELATIONS AMONG INDIVIDUALS can take shape according to a variety of patterns; at one extreme they are based upon pure love, as bestowed by the mother upon her child, and at the other, upon unmitigated fear and hatred as felt by the caveman confronted with a stranger. Relations among human groups are similar, except that they are never based on pure love and only in a few cases on pure fear and hatred. The two extreme types of group relations are often called co-operation, where there is no conflict, and fight, where the conflict is so acute that it makes accommodation unthinkable and the elimination of the opponent the only worthwhile objective. The majority of situations fall between these two and may be called competition. There, conflict exists but is not absolute, because it is tempered by some community of interest, and often ends in compromise.

Relations among states are governed both by the nature of states and that of international society. It may be recalled that the main characteristics of states are that they are the supreme form of human organization, that they recognize no superior and are governed by self-interest. Accordingly international society (which will be discussed in Chapters 6 and 7) does not exercise authoritative power over them, although it does prescribe certain rules of behaviour. If social progress is measured by the evolution of co-operation and of peaceful means for the resolution of conflicts, international society is still very primitive.

Inter-state behaviour exhibits every stage of conflict, from constant references to power politics and threats of violence to actual war which, in our century, has become increasingly more dangerous. The logical conclusion of the present situation is that this Hobbesian starting point could lead to a form of social contract which would bring to an end this unbearable state of affairs.

The ferocious nature of the two World Wars led to several attempts to eliminate violence: the League of Nations Covenant, the Kellogg Pact, many agreements and declarations, and, lately, the United Nations Charter. Although these approaches varied and were interpreted in differing ways, they did not, as a rule, constitute a departure from the fundamental structure of the international society of states governed by self-interest. They merely accepted the fact that these states were so adversely affected by the danger of recurrent wars, that this very self-interest demanded that violence should be eliminated, or, as became current in the language of international organization, that aggression should be prevented. The attempts to eliminate violence did not prevent the Second World War or decrease the danger of a third, nuclear war.

The new institutions and methods not only expressed the idea that a fight to the finish, to eliminate the opponent, was undesirable and therefore scarcely thinkable, but also reinforced this idea by institutionalizing it. During the last war, despite the fundamental nature of the Nazi menace, the United Nations did not seriously contemplate the complete and perpetual elimination of Germany from the international scene; neither do the Americans and the Russians necessarily aspire to mutual annihilation—they would be satisfied with a change in each other's social and political systems.

The first attempts to eliminate the use of force having failed, men have sought more effective methods of accommodation by analysing more thoroughly the nature of international conflicts. Lately the Americans have been developing ingenious although so far inconclusive studies based on the 'theory of games', and have been analysing the complexities of the policy of deterrence. The following paragraphs are based on the ideas of a prominent theoretician of deterrence, the Harvard Professor Thomas C. Schelling, in *The Strategy of Conflict*.

The starting point of his argument is that pure conflict, war to the finish, would be so mutually damaging that limiting warfare to minimize damage, or coercing the other side by threatening war rather than by waging it, has become expedient for both sides and has opened possibilities of accommodation. There is not only mutual opposition but also mutual dependence. Victory in the conflict is not strictly competitive, not necessarily at the cost of the other side. Conflict situations are now essentially bargaining situations, since they combine a divergence of interests with the powerful common interest that the outcome should not be destructive to both sides; success means the avoidance of war.

In order to transcend the emotional difficulties of the cold war, Professor Schelling recommends the study of conflict in other, less emotionally charged and less complex relations. Undoubtedly the combination of conflicting and common interests, although in different proportions, occurs among non-enemies, and deterrence has its place even among friends and allies. In 1956 when the Poles were standing up to the Russians, their attitude was determined by a combination of the physical threat from Russia and their interest in retaining Soviet support which is indispensable for the maintenance of the communist regime and of the Western Territories acquired from Germany. When the Americans unsuccessfully tried to force the French to ratify the European Defence Community in 1954, they stressed common strategic interests but also hinted at the possibility of an 'agonizing reappraisal' in case of failure. Gang-warfare offers an interesting parallel. Like states, outlaws lack enforceable legal systems, constantly invoke the threat of violence, and ultimately engage in it although they have an interest in avoiding it. Hence they provide illustration for such international moves as disarmament and disengagement, surprise attack, retaliation and its threat, appeasement and loss of face, or the unreliability of the widespread alliances and agreements.

The great advantage of this analysis lies in its realism; it takes into account both the conflict and the community of interests, as they exist together in life, while at the same time it shifts attention to the more promising elements of community. Provided each side acts rationally and fully understands the situation, not only as it appears to itself but also as it appears to the other side, the chances of accommodation greatly increase. The fact that the Russians have been translating into Russian the major American analyses and have thus had an opportunity to become acquainted

with all the subtleties of American views, offers considerable hope
that accommodation may become easier even in the cold war.

Finally, we speak of co-operation, where the problem lies not in
the identification of common goals and of the methods of reaching them, but rather in the achievement of these goals. This
interaction, in which no conflict is involved, does not, properly
speaking, come into the ambits of politics which centres on conflict
and power, but rather into that of administration. But administration is not only the outcome of successful politics but also
offers a method of resolving conflict situations, especially when
they are not acute.

If an international agreement about basic goals and methods is
ever reached, it will be a sufficient foundation for the establishment of a world government. Obviously we are very remote from
such a state of affairs today, but this does not prevent states from
co-operating, in the narrower meaning of the word here employed, namely, interacting without conflict. From the establishment of the Geodetic Union in 1864, international organizations
have multiplied to over 1,200, including some 150 inter-governmental ones; many important activities are carried out under the
auspices of the United Nations and of its Specialized Agencies.
The so-called 'functional co-operation' embraces wide areas of
international life, but is completely successful only when it does
not affect power relations. Thus the peaceful progress of international postal administration through the Universal Postal
Union strongly contrasts with the turbulent relations in the field
of telecommunications, first the telegraph and now the radio. The
reasons are not far to seek—postal exchange is not nearly so
strategically important as telecommunications.

Although relatively unimportant from the angle of power relations, international functional co-operation is never fully
divorced from them. It offers two interesting prospects. First, as
institutions multiply and evolve highly complex methods of co-
operation, technical difficulties involved in implementing any
political agreement are being reduced and no issue is likely to be
wrecked by them. Even such a complex problem as phased disarmament which would offer no sizeable advantage to either side
during any phase, can be adequately solved provided the political
decision is made. Second, if the network of the slender ties of
functional co-operation continues to increase at the present rate,

it may eventually resemble the system of threads with which the Lilliputians tied down Gulliver—although singly the strands were weak and insignificant, their total strength was sufficient for their purpose. It is conceivable that in some future time states will depend on functional international co-operation to satisfy so many minor human needs that eventually the disruption of such co-operation through violence will become unthinkable. This approach to peace need not exclude other approaches.

The problem of power enters into all types of international relations. Wars, competition, and co-operation, all involve power —the first two military power, though in competition it is used only to deter; all three contain non-military elements. A state which is devoid of resources and organization can neither compete nor co-operate successfully with other states. Hence the logical next step is to discuss the meaning of state power.

The Nature of National Power

All politics, by definition, revolve around the exercise and the pursuit of power, but in international politics power is considerably more in evidence and less circumscribed than in domestic politics, and hence this field is often described as 'power politics'. The word 'power' is used in many connotations—we speak about Great and Small Powers, about the balance of power, etc. The conspicuous role played by power in international relations has led to a school of interpretation centring around it and also to a reaction in the form of a condemnation of power politics, based on the expectation that power can be eliminated and replaced by international institutions.

Neither extreme approach is fully satisfactory. Although power plays a central role in international politics, it is fundamentally an instrument for the achievement of national values. International politics are determined not only by the power wielded by the various states but also, or rather, by the values held by these states. The concept of national interest which governs state behaviour is not limited to power considerations alone.

The school of thought seeking to eliminate power is even less realistic. It is based on the historical experiences of the Anglo-Saxon countries in the nineteenth century. In Britain, power relations at that time became obscured by the apparent divorce of economics from politics and by the temporary security of the country which led to the illusion of a rule of law in international society; in the United States aloofness from the game of European power politics was not only an aspiration but a tangible fact. The moralistic condemnation of power stemming from these experiences, and the exaggerated hope that international institutions would replace power politics, could not stand the test of the totalitarian challenge in the thirties. A more balanced attitude prevails now. It is futile to attempt a moral evaluation of power in the abstract—it can serve both good and evil purposes. Power certainly cannot be done away with, and our problem is not how to eliminate it but how to control it, to confine it within legitimate channels.

Not all the major problems of power in domestic politics require discussion also within the international context. That states wield power is accepted as a fact apart from its possible justification through theories of sovereignty derived from God or the people; in the international context, the organic theories explaining power in terms of its function, or the ends it is serving, ultimately boil down to self-preservation.

It is not easy to explain the meaning of the word 'power'. In the first instance, a distinction must be made between the word as it is employed in various spheres. In mathematics 'power' is a technical term meaning the product arising from the continued multiplication of a number by itself; in physics it means the rate of transfer of energy, as in work done by an engine; in human relations it is now generally understood as a relational phenomenon, not a thing that one possesses, it denotes *the capacity to produce intended effects*; specifically political power is not power over nature, a material, or oneself, but *over the minds and actions of other men.*

The concept of power in human relations is too complex to permit the precision with which it can be used in other domains. Even in inter-personal relations many interconnected elements must be taken into account. Cleopatra's nose is one famous example of the exercise of power—the argument being that had it not been for Cleopatra's beauty Antony could have rallied himself and successfully opposed Octavian. But apart from beauty Cleopatra was also endowed with mental and emotional attributes, and her power cannot possibly be understood without an analysis of the whole complex relationship between her and Antony.

In international relations the concept of power is often befogged by two fallacies. It is understood in a predominantly or even exclusively military sense, as power to wage war. This may have been roughly true about the pre-nuclear era, but the definition is obviously inappropriate to our own age when, against the background of mutual deterrence, other non-military elements of power are increasingly significant. Moreover, whereas military power remains extremely important in relations between *governments*, it is not much use in the now frequent direct appeals to the *people* of other states. Allied with this is the fallacy that power is measurable and quantifiable just because you can add up and compare such things as the numbers of soldiers under arms, the tonnage of battleships, the potential of the steel industry serving war needs, etc.

In order to explain power in international relations in its broadest meaning it is convenient to distinguish between those relations that include an element of coercion and those that do not. In fact it may be advisable to accept, as Professor Sprout does,[1] the military connotations of the term power and to limit it to actions and situations having within them an element of coercion. The other, non-coercive aspects of power can be called influence. It is unfortunate but symptomatic of our preoccupation with coercion that our language lacks a positive term for these aspects. Perhaps we cannot find it because the coercive and non-coercive elements cannot be clearly separated. Gentle, persuasive diplomacy works much more efficiently if backed by the guns and aeroplanes of the state, although these need never be mentioned; coercive elements, if used starkly, are not very useful since they can lead to desperate opposition. The use of force, actual physical coercion, is not a logical exercise of power. On the contrary, as shown by the Soviet intervention in Czechoslovakia in August 1968, it shows that power is deficient and is no longer accepted as insuperable.

State power involves several important elements usually referred to as capabilities, which will be discussed in turn, but these elements do not add up to a full explanation; indeed, the fact that some of them can be quantitatively expressed should not

[1] H. and M. Sprout, *The Foundations of International Politics*, 1962.

mislead us into thinking of power as a quantifiable entity. The power of states is better understood through their actions than through the analysis of static elements; as the etymological origin of the word in several languages (*dynamis, potentia*) indicates, it has a potential character, and Professor Sprout goes so far as to call the combination of coercive and non-coercive elements 'potential'.

Finally, the point must be made that, although power plays a role in most international transactions and is central in many, it is not an ingredient in all. We speak then of 'non-political' or 'technical' matters. It is often impossible to agree about the political or non-political character of an issue, but the distinction is very important. It is found at the centre of the recurrent controversies between the United States and its allies regarding trade with Communist China, which have been referred to previously; trade, if regarded as predominantly technical, non-political, is governed by quite different considerations from trade considered as political, as a factor which can strengthen a hostile state.

It is the will of states alone that determines the political character of issues. Anything which can even remotely affect the vital interests of the state is political. When it becomes the subject of an international dispute, the state refuses to regard the dispute as legal, i.e. suitable for being deceived by an impartial arbiter; it reserves the right to secure terms of settlement which are acceptable to itself, in the last resort even by force. The character of activities does not fully determine their non-political nature even when they are so obviously humanitarian as the abolition of slavery or of forced labour; they become pronouncedly political when directed against a specific state in which these institutions still exist. The identity of the states involved is just as important as the character of the activity. Obviously Switzerland is much less likely than the United States or the Soviet Union to regard her trade issues as political; furthermore, Swiss trade with a small neutral country like Eire is less likely to give rise to political issues than her trade with one of the Superpowers.

One of the most important classifications of states, into Great and Small Powers, is based upon gradations in power. The vocabulary of international politics includes also such terms as middle, or weak, or world, or superpowers. No clear objective criteria can be evolved to decide to which category a given state belongs. Up to a point the estimates are impressionistic and states tend to rank themselves higher than other states would do, in much the same way as individuals tend to classify themselves as belonging to a higher social class than objective sociologists would allow them.

The traditionally important category of Great Powers can be regarded as a self-perpetuating club, the members of which recognize one another as being Great Powers. Sometimes members drop out, usually as a result of military defeat, as Sweden did early in the eighteenth century; sometimes new members are added after having proved their prowess, as did the United States in the war against Spain in 1898 or Japan through her victory over Russia in 1904–5. The position of the Great Powers was extremely important in the nineteenth century when they were acting as the guardians of international order in the Concert of Europe. It was to some extent preserved when they were allotted permanent seats in the Councils of the League of Nations and the United Nations.

Since 1945 the distinction has not retained much of its utility. First, the United States and the Soviet Union have risen to power so great that it cannot possibly be matched by other states. These two states are often called Superpowers—they are the only two Powers with substantial nuclear weapons sufficient for mutual annihilation, and with world-wide interests. The Superpowers are thus simultaneously nuclear Powers and world Powers.

The category of the five permanent members of the United Nations Security Council includes three other states—The United Kingdom, France, and China. The first two of these states, although very remote from the position of the two Superpowers, come somewhat closer to it than other states. Both are nuclear Powers—Britain actually possesses operational nuclear weapons while France is actively developing them. Also, although their colonial empires have all but vanished, they have retained sufficient interests and influence outside Europe to make them, if not world Powers, at least Powers with broader than purely regional interests. Nationalist China, which occupies a seat in the United Nations, is a Great Power in name only. The other reasonable contenders for a Great Power status are Communist China, India, Western Germany, and Japan. The nature and justification of their claims can be best explained in the light of a discussion of the elements of power or capabilities.

Capabilities

Although an analysis of capabilities seems indispensable for the study of international relations, the warning must be repeated that the mechanical sum total of these elements does not take us very far in explaining the actual amount of power wielded by a state. Despite the great progress lately made in statistical analysis, the assessment by Francis Bacon still stands:

The greatness of an estate, in bulk and territory, does fall under measure; and the greatness of finances and revenue does fall under computation. The population may appear by musters, and the number and greatness of cities by cards and maps; but yet there is not anything, amongst civil affairs, more subject to error than the right valuation and true judgement concerning the power and forces of an estate.

Power can be realistically estimated only in action, and discussion of capabilities can take us no further than the understanding of the state's potential, or its capacity for such action.

Some general points should be borne in mind whenever one analyses any particular element of power of any specific state. First, all power elements are relative to those possessed by other states, especially neighbours and possible rivals and opponents. The statement that Britain has a population of 53 million is meaningless in terms of power-relations unless we compare it with the populations of her larger European neighbours (to which it is roughly equal) and those of her Superpowers (which are much larger). Second, mere quantities are fairly meaningless. Population figures must be broken up according to age, sex, skills, education, etc.; numbers of aeroplanes according to range, speed, weapon-carrying capacity, etc.

Third, single capabilities play their part in the complex totality of the state's power and can be evaluated only against this background. No one element will suffice if the state is deficient in others; for instance, military power alone is inadequate unless it is backed by sufficient population and industrial resources to keep pace with technological advance and to replace possible losses.

Whenever a state has a surplus of an element of power, over and above actual and likely future needs, this surplus is only marginally relevant as a remote strategic reserve. Thus the United States is not rendered much stronger by the capacity of its steel production, well above the military and civilian needs. The large numbers of China's or India's populations are in one way an element of strength but in another of weakness, since neither country can adequately feed them. In fact, what is usually an element of power can become a liability—for instance if a state deficient in other elements possesses large deposits of rare fissionable materials which make it a coveted prize for the Great Powers.

Fourth, capabilities may be utilized either more or less efficiently. It is conceivable, though not quite certain, that although Soviet steel production both in absolute quantities and per capita is much lower than that of the United States, it may be equally adequate for maintaining the Soviet power-position because it is always used to capacity and because Soviet consumer industry needs are considerably lower. The power-value of a detachment of troops or weapons varies according to the strategic doctrine they are serving; thus during the Nazi attack on France in May 1940, a tank in the hands of the German Command was strategically much more valuable than a mechanically equivalent tank in the hands of the French.

Fifth, since we live in an era of uniquely rapid technological advance, the relative importance of the various capabilities is incessantly changing. Oil has replaced coal as the main source of fuel and may itself be replaced in the future by uranium; uranium will lose its value if nuclear processes are mastered to the point of releasing energy through fusion in which fissionable material is unnecessary. Weapons are incessantly going out of date—submarines have rendered useless capital ships, and ballistic missiles are gradually supplanting manned aeroplanes. It is not only technology that changes. A profound disturbance in power-relations can arise not only from the evolution of new raw materials or of new weapons but from the less tangible though equally important changes in the efficiency of government or in the morale of the people.

Sixth, the aspect of readiness must not be neglected. Even in the past all strategists readily distinguished between soldiers under arms and soldiers who had to be mobilized, or between operational ships and those laid up. Today, in the era of push-button warfare, there is an even greater difference between a bomber which requires a few hours to be ready for flying, a bomber kept on the alert, and one actually airborne. The first would be valueless in a surprise attack, and the value of the airborne bomber would be obviously much higher than that of one merely on the alert which, through numerous causes, may not become operational in time.

Consequently analysis cannot be limited to data available on the present or the recent past but must perforce include an estimate of trends both in the elements of power currently considered important and in those likely to become so in the future. Here the main problem is how to make the necessary distinctions between reliable statistics and estimates, and between their timing. For example, if we compute the Soviet productive capacity of nuclear missiles, we still do not know how many missiles they have actually produced, since they may not be able or wish to use their capacity to the full. While most strategic analyses centre around inter-continental ballistic missiles the destructive power of biological and chemical weapons is not compared; simultaneously the obsolete manned bombers still dominate the skies. A comparison of the American and the Soviet nuclear striking abilities in 1950, 1960, and 1970 would produce vastly different results; therefore any comparison must employ statistics and estimates strictly comparable in time.

State power can be broken up into many identifiable factors. Most writers distinguish five groups: the demographic, the geographical, the economic, the organizational and the psychological-social, and the international-strategic.

Population. Undoubtedly the power of a state is related to the size of its population. Although the correlation is not absolute, it is valid to the extent that no state with a small population can become a Great Power. The two Superpowers have large populations, the Soviet Union over 230 million and the United States nearly 200 million; the most populous states, China with possibly as many as 750 million, and India with over 500 million, are serious aspirants for Great Power status although they do not in any way approximate the power-position of the two less populous Superpowers. The sudden growth of the population of Europe, especially of Britain in the last three centuries, led to the building of colonial empires but, in the different conditions of our century, a similar expansion of the populations of Latin America, Asia, and Africa cannot possibly lead to strictly comparable results. An estimate of the trends in population development is indispensable for making long-range power calculations. The highly industrialized western states, which have reached a fairly stable equilibrium between the birth- and the death-rates, are likely to increase within the next few decades at a much slower rate than other societies in which the death-rates are being suddenly reduced whereas the birth-rates continue high.

Bare numbers do not tell us much. We must ascertain the proportion of the population in the crucial age-group of 20–35 years, which is both the most productive and the best capable of bearing arms. Comparison of this age-group in different countries requires further refinements according to the utilization of women for both tasks. Whereas during the last war the Soviet Union employed women in industrial production and to some extent also for military service, the Germans did not; hence the correct comparison is that of German man-power and Soviet man- plus 'women-power'. Furthermore, the extent of literacy, education, and industrial skills can prove decisive. In 1942 the Germans could challenge the Russians because the population of the Soviet Union, although three times more numerous, was inferior to them in most of these respects. Today, this not being so, the sheer weight of Russian numbers makes such a challenge unthinkable.

Geography. Geography is so prominent in the make-up of the territorial state that some thinkers, the 'geopoliticians', have been seeking the full explanation of foreign policy in geographical influences. Needless to say, like any other explanation which attempts to reduce a complex reality to one single factor, 'geopolitics' cannot be accepted as an adequate theory even though the geographical element of power counts for much.

Undoubtedly a certain correlation between power and the size of the state's territory does exist, although it is considerably less pronounced than the correlation with the size of the population. The largest state, the Soviet Union, which measures over $8\frac{1}{2}$ million square miles, is very powerful but not more so than the

United States which covers just under 3 million. Despite her small area (just over 100,000 square miles when including the whole of Ireland) Britain managed to play a leading role in world politics and to build up the greatest colonial empire. In fact, where vast waste tracts of land divided the centres of population, size can be a handicap until adequate communications have been developed; Australia, for example, is not strengthened by the barren waste of her interior.

Shape, location, and topography are all important. For strategic and administrative purposes a state should be compact with a capital more or less in the centre, as France is, whereas an elongated state like Czechoslovakia or Chile is difficult both to defend and to govern. The 'geopoliticians' have attributed to location a decisive influence, and indeed much of the turbulent history of Germany or Poland is due to their position in the midst of the Great European Plain, whereas, in her insular isolation, Britain was able to develop the foundations of a world empire, while Spain and Portugal, the Scandinavian countries or Japan sometimes effectively withdrew from the mainstream of power politics. Modern technology has reduced the significance of topography and the desirability of such 'natural frontiers' as mountain-ranges or rivers, but location remains important.

Finally, climate greatly influences the produce of the land and the character of its people. The great centres of power have so far arisen only in the moderate zone, between 20 and 60 degrees North.

Economics. The economic basis of modern states is paramount both in peace and war. It determines the living conditions and the well-being of their peoples and provides them with the wherewithal for a successful foreign policy; it also serves as the foundation for an armaments industry and is, as a rule, decisive in war.

The Gross National Product (G.N.P.) is useful as a general index of economic strength particularly when broken down on the per capita basis and supplemented by an estimate of the growth rate. Unfortunately national figures are computed in vastly different ways, and are therefore not strictly comparable.

Usually two components are distinguished in the economic element: natural resources and industrial production. Again comparisons are inaccurate but nevertheless quite telling as general indicators of strength.

Whenever evaluating the economic elements of power one must bear in mind the distinction between capacity and actual production. Although the Soviet steel production capacity is not much more than half that of the United States, it is generally fully utilized while, owing to economic fluctuations, the American capacity is generally worked only partly; hence the discrepancy between the quantities of steel actually produced by the two countries is considerably less than that between their capacities. Moreover, while much of American steel is put to a marginally social use, for instance to make the cars even bigger, it is for power purposes much less effectively used than Soviet steel which is made into weapons and essential consumer goods. Against that, the quality of the product must be borne in mind; defective end-products which are useless or only partially useful are likely to be less frequent in the competitive American system than in a communist society where dire penalties threaten factories which fail to produce their allotted quotas.

If a state is deficient in a raw material or productive capacity, one must investigate how it can overcome the shortage through stockpiling or imports, and on what economic and strategic conditions, or how a substitute could be discovered through technological advance. For instance, one of the strategically important materials which the United States lacks is rubber. For a long time the Americans were dependent on imports from South-East Asia, which put them into a strategically dangerous position owing to the distances involved; to meet a sudden emergency they stockpiled considerable quantities of rubber, and finally evolved methods of producing artificial rubber which is in some respects superior to the natural product.

Only the two Superpowers approach self-sufficiency and even they are dependent on the importation of some raw materials. In 1960 the United States imported some seventy key materials totalling about 15 per cent of its entire raw material consumption, and it was estimated that these imports would rise further. The Soviet Union imports considerably less now and is more likely to find at home additional raw materials to meet the needs of increased industrial production in the future.

Strategically important raw materials fall into three groups with a certain overlap: fuels (coal, oil, natural gas, and fissile materials); metals (especially iron to which coal must be added for steel production; copper; metals used to harden steel such as chromium, manganese, and nickel; bauxite, lead, zinc, tin, titanium, silver, etc.); and agricultural produce, subdivided into food and industrial crops. In industrial production steel output, which is the basis of all heavy industry, and particularly of the production of weapons, usually receives much prominence; the chemical and the electronics industries are now important in all advanced economies.

Clearly, the two Superpowers lead the world and the only combination of states which could match them is the European Economic Community, if it is enlarged by Britain. Apart from these, only Japan is highly industrialized although she lacks raw materials, while China and also India are seriously set upon the path of industrialization. Economic growth has now become the major goal of all states which are appropriately referred to in this connection as under-developed or developing. From the point of view of power-relations, states already industrialized are in a much better position than others. Not only can they supply more weapons for their armies and more goods for their people, but they have a much better chance of crossing the threshold beyond which economic growth becomes a self-perpetuating process, as it is in the West and in the Soviet Union. In the long run, as more and more producers compete for raw materials, although greater deposits of these are constantly found and more efficiently exploited and although substitutes often become possible, it is conceivable that states controlling rare raw materials will be in the most powerful position, able to command in exchange all that they require.

Governmental and military organization. The potential elements of power are utilized according to how efficiently they are organized; hence the importance of government. Sudden changes in the power position of a state can be entirely due to a change of government, as happened in Germany, when the Nazis replaced the Weimar Republic, or in China, when the Communist Government replaced the Nationalist one.

The contemporary types of authoritarian and democratic governments differ in their respective advantages and disadvantages. An authoritarian government can override the wishes of its people, and hence can act with speed, and, at least in the short run, with efficiency. A democratic government must persuade its people first. This is often a slow and difficult process, sometimes to no avail, but it has the offsetting advantage that the more active consent of the people ensures the stability of the government and enables it to withstand stress. If we compare the systems in contemporary China and India, we find that the Chinese Government was the more able to mobilize the whole population and to divert scarce resources to economic development but became involved in a devastating 'Cultural Revolution'. The much less efficient and less ruthless Indian Government may have done quite as well although it is facing severe economic and minority challenges.

How significant is the quality of the civil service, is demonstrated by the comparison of newly emancipated colonial territories. Territories which inherited a reasonable civil service, such as Ghana or Nigeria, fared, at least at first, much better than countries in which it had broken down, as Indonesia or the Belgian Congo. For international relations, particularly relevant is the quality of diplomacy. It is generally agreed that Britain's power is greatly enhanced by the quality and experience of her diplomacy.

Although, as has been mentioned, its role is often exaggerated, military power is an essential condition for the survival of the state in war and also for its prestige in peacetime. Comparisons of military organization are confusing since we must bear in mind at least three separate military elements: the deterrent; the so-called conventional weapons, traditionally divided into air, naval, and army branches; and strategic doctrine. Moreover, the respective importance of the three is constantly changing. During the immediate post-war years the Americans greatly overrated nuclear weapons to the detriment of conventional ones. Even now possession of nuclear weapons is a major condition for Great Power status and nuclear equilibrium is the major objective of the two Superpowers, but what will happen if several other states follow Britain and France in developing their individual nuclear weapons?

The value of strategic doctrine lies in choosing military power of the right sort. Thus French military doctrine in the inter-war period can be blamed for the defeat in 1940, since the French were prepared for a static trench warfare of the First World War type and not for the mobile warfare of the Second World War. Today the major problems lie in determining the proportion of resources to be devoted to nuclear weapons necessary for deterrence and for a nuclear war, and to conventional weapons useful in minor conflicts. Also the differences between the strategy of deterrence and that to be employed in the minor clashes of the cold war, such as subversion or infiltration, require definition.

The proportion of the G.N.P. devoted to military ends indicates the intensity of the military effort and offers a clue to the prospects of its durability. In 1966 the Russians devoted to it about 8·9 per cent of their G.N.P., the Americans some 9·2 per cent. The latter, however, not only enjoy a much higher national product but also do not fully utilize their industrial capacity. Hence sustained or even increased armament programmes would not be particularly onerous for them; on the contrary, they would mean a more efficient use of facilities and less unemployment. On the other hand, the Russians are showing definite signs of economic strain. It is obvious that they could very usefully employ a large proportion of their defence expenditure for urgent investment needs and consumption.

Comparison of actual military strength is highly technical and need not be pursued here beyond the conclusion that both the Americans and the Russians have more than sufficient 'second-strike capability', i.e. enough nuclear weapons to inflict serious damage on the opponent even after having been subject to a devastating nuclear attack; the power-value of the British and the French deterrents is highly controversial. Likewise inconclusive is the comparison of conventional military resources. While we can count the troops and weapons classified according to their striking power, the intangible element of the political attitudes of both the soldiers and the civilians must not be neglected. Support, although often enforced, of the native people for communist guerillas in South-east Asia multiplies the power-value of the numerically small active communists; nationalist, anti-Russian sentiments may greatly reduce the reliability and hence the power-value of the troops of the eastern European countries which belong to the Soviet bloc. Certainly the Czech troops could be scarcely expected to fight whole-heartedly on behalf of the Warsaw Pact.

Psychological-social elements. This category embraces all the less tangible elements of power which cannot be easily bracketed within any of the preceding categories.

It is necessary to distinguish the social system from the governmental one. A people united and homogeneous are obviously much stronger than one disunited and heterogeneous. Any major rifts, whether racial, national, religious, or of any other kind, detract, at least potentially, from the power of the state because it may not be able to muster the whole strength of its population whenever factional interests clash. This somewhat intangible element augments the power of the United Kingdom with its stable social system, and casts doubts on the ultimate strength of the Soviet Union where important national, religious, and ideological differences are known to exist. The racial disturbances in the United States have seriously detracted from its power potential.

Then there is the factor often referred to as morale. Morale describes the extent to which the people support their leaders, believe in the superiority of their state and in the rightness of their cause. It depends upon a combination of circumstances and the quality of leadership and can be subject to frequent and sometimes sudden flunctuations. Thus the French morale was much higher than the British one throughout the sixties but was severely shaken by the students' riots and the general strike in 1968.

A more permanent intangible element is national character. Although the stereotypes of national character can be grossly misleading, there is some foundation for the observation that different nations tend to develop their own peculiar ways of thinking and acting, some of which are more useful than others for the power of the state; there can be little doubt about the advantages of German industriousness or the disadvantages of Polish unruliness in the past. Analysis of national character does not, however, take us very far. First of all, national character, although much more stable than morale, does change. In the seventeenth century the English were reputed to be the most turbulent nation in Europe and in the eighteenth the Germans the most romantic and peaceful, but quite justifiably neither reputation holds today. Second, it is notoriously difficult to agree on what national character actually is or how useful are some of its features. It is fairly easy to catalogue the differences between the

Americans and the Russians and to arrive at the conclusion that their national characters are diametrically opposed. It is not much more difficult to list the similarities due to the common factors of size and concentration on material achievements, and to arrive at the opposite conclusion.

Prestige is derived from some features of society that involve power and from others that do not, but is an element of power in itself because it helps the state to obtain the desired social response from others. It is built upon the image formed by others of the state's qualities, an image often having little in common with reality—especially when the supposed qualities are merely a matter of the past. The qualities that count for the purpose of prestige vary from period to period, and states tend to evolve their own individual methods for enhancing their reputations.

Military, today particularly nuclear power, is a sound foundation for international prestige. So is economic strength, though here prestige ambiguously embraces several elements. There is the element of economic strength as a basis for and supplement to military power; as the ability to provide largesse abroad; as a testimony to the soundness of the ideological foundations of society. In the last-mentioned respect, the Russians have been scoring because their centrally planned economy can boast of one of the highest rates of economic growth sustained over many years. One should not, however, forget the frequently unacknowledged prestige accruing to the United States for its indisputably highest standard of living and for all the glossy gadgets its citizens enjoy. Despite all the incidental harm Hollywood films may be doing to American prestige, they ensure that the whole world is familiar with the American standard of living.

In our age which is so acutely aware of human rights, social justice has become important for the reputation of a state. Infringements of freedom, or of other rights of the individual, become dark blotches on the escutcheon of national society, whether they are forced labour camps in Siberia or race discrimination and interracial violence in the United States.

International strategic position. State power is determined not only by the combination of all the above-mentioned domestic elements of power but also by the position of the state in the world. No state, not even the Superpowers, is fully self-supporting; all depend on military allies, on friends in diplomacy, on suppliers and markets in economics. All the elements of power in their possession can be considerably augmented by outside support. Such support is highly desirable, perhaps indispensable, but its value and cost require careful computation. First, the ultimate command of the resources which can be called upon from abroad remains in foreign hands: the promised troops may be refused at the last minute, the expected economic aid may be stopped, the raw materials may not be delivered. Excessive reliance on uncertain support is obviously dangerous. Second, there are the drawbacks of cost and risk. The concessions necessary to ensure the reliability of an ally may be so great as to reduce the power of the state in relation to this ally, although the alliance strengthens its power in relation to other states. To take the example of American alliances since the last war—they certainly have proved costly and are, with the exception of NATO, both ineffective and precarious. While they have been concluded and are being maintained in the belief that they increase American power, the contrary could be argued about alignments such as that with South Vietnam.

The value of political support short of an alliance, or of benevolent neutrality, is obvious in the deliberations of the General Assembly. The United States and the Soviet Union vie in their efforts to secure the goodwill of the numerically preponderant Afro-Asian bloc; much of Soviet diplomatic power in the United Nations comes from the anti-colonial and therefore anti-Western attitudes of this bloc. A state concerned in a matter coming up on the agenda of the General Assembly is compelled to make the rounds of other members, and the isolation of such states as South Africa or Portugal greatly reduces their power.

5

Instruments and Techniques of State Interaction

Some General Distinctions

UP TO A POINT historical events are unique; hence the broader the scope of our study the more difficult does generalization become. It is reasonably easy to analyse the relations of one country with another in any given period but increasingly less so when relations include additional countries and spread over longer periods of time. Subsequent remarks are related to the whole modern international society in a broad historical setting and so, by necessity, they cannot be very precise.

In different areas and periods the intensity of international relations greatly varies. While Mesopotamia became the stage of ramified international relations some millennia before our era, the remote Himalayan realms of Tibet and Nepal remained isolated until this century. One cannot appreciate the foreign policy of any state without some idea of how involved it is in its relations with other states—today the United States and the Soviet Union are obviously the most active countries, while many neutrals are trying with varying degrees of success to stay out of the mainstream of power politics. Major issues of foreign policy centre around involvement, for instance to what extent should Britain or France pursue their policies as nuclear Powers, as active members of NATO, and as senior partners in networks of relationships with their ex-colonies?

Traditionally, states have been trying to escape what they considered excessive involvement through isolationism and neutrality. Isolationism is definitely on the wane while neutrality has now completely changed its meaning. Isolationism, meaning a deliberate withdrawal from international relations, is no longer possible on the basis of geographical isolation, as pursued by China and Japan until the incursion of European influence. Britain's 'splendid isolation' in the nineteenth century did not really amount to non-involvement; on the contrary, Britain actively participated in all major European conflicts except the Franco-Prussian War. The term merely described the operation of the balance of power system which did not demand from Britain continuous participation but only sporadic interventions. Likewise the 'splendid isolation' of the United States was to some extent mythical. The Americans were extremely active in the Western Hemisphere and closely watched European politics but, owing to the protection of the friendly British Navy, they could refrain from taking part in them directly.

Fifty years ago neutrality was a strictly legal concept describing non-participation in war, which confers certain rights and imposes certain duties on the neutral state. Today it has generally assumed the meaning of non-alignment, of not being committed to either major bloc, and of refusing to participate in their systems of alliances. The term applies to a state's attitude to the cold war alone. The non-aligned states endeavour to avoid commitment to either the Russians or the Americans but they are in varying degrees involved in quite intensive international relations outside this context.

It is necessary to take into account both the attitude of the state to international order as a whole and to other single states and blocs. Some states like to preserve the stability of the international order which, they feel, serves their national interest; they are the defenders of the 'status quo' (*status quo ante bellum* is a diplomatic term describing in peace treaties the state of affairs which had existed before the beginning of hostilities). Other states, feeling that the order is against their national interest and that they would gain by changing it, are usually described as 'revisionist' Powers. These positive or negative attitudes to the existing international order vary in intensity and determination. Not all supporters of the *status quo* are equally ready to defend it, and likewise not all revisionist states are equally determined to strive for the downfall of the existing order. States vary greatly in their attitudes to friends, potential enemies, and neutrals.

Inevitably they are influenced by them in their choice of instruments and techniques.

Such choices are partly determined by the availability of the various power elements: a state militarily weak is naturally inclined to develop its foreign relations with the aid of non-military instruments and techniques; a state economically weak is limited in its choice of economic instruments and techniques. The choice, however, cannot be made at the will of the state, according to a rational appraisal of its attitudes to the other party and of its power-position. Some inescapable influences arise within the international environment—opportunities and challenges in every field change with the lapse of time, international fashions and the 'rules of the game' governing international intercourse are not static. Thus post-war American foreign policy has been justly criticized for its excessive reliance upon nuclear weapons in which the United States is strong, despite the fact that these weapons are useless in the majority of issues and that the major communist challenges have gradually shifted to the ideological and the economic fields. France and Britain learnt only through the failure of their Suez expedition in 1956 that in the mid-twentieth century armed intervention could be undertaken only with the support of at least one of the Superpowers or of the United Nations. The western Powers still rather pathetically complain that they cannot cope with communist-inspired subversion.

Until the First World War international relations were conducted with other governments alone, but since then relations with the people of other states have been growing in importance. Consequently instruments and techniques suitable for inter-governmental relations have been supplemented and to a certain extent displaced by those suitable for approaching these people. Often dilemmas arise. For instance, when determining their relations with unfriendly communist governments in eastern Europe, the Americans sometimes helped them in their economic difficulties in the hope of securing their goodwill and of weakening their allegiance to the Soviet bloc (this was called detachment). The alternative was to appeal to the people of these countries to overthrow their governments and replace them with governments which would be more friendly to the United States and would therefore qualify for assistance (this was called subversion). Obviously these two policies were incompatible.

Foreign policy is not only directed towards other governments but can also use them as instruments. One of the characteristics of the post-war period has been 'aggression by proxy'. The Russians never use their troops except within their immediate sphere of influence and the many communist-inspired disturbances in the world are engineered by foreign Communists employed as instruments of Soviet foreign policy. Only the Yugoslav and the Chinese revolutions were genuinely national.

The influence of international organization has been steadily growing. The far-reaching prohibition of the use or threat of force in the conduct of international relations, which is embodied in the Charter of the United Nations, is not always observed but exercises a considerable influence on the behaviour of states. In general, other things not being too unequal, states will tend to choose instruments and techniques compatible with the Charter and likely to find approval with international public opinion as expressed in the General Assembly. Of course the degree of deference varies with the single states and according to the significance of the issues involved.

In the interaction among states there are no clear-cut divisions between friends and foes, between persuasion and coercion. In most cases relations include varying, even conflicting, elements—a threat of coercion occasionally creeps into the most amicable relationship, and even ardent ideological opponents may find it possible to compromise in matters of trade. Peace does not preclude the existence of conflict, even of quite an acute nature, nor does war mean complete severance of non-coercive relations. All the instruments and techniques of international intercourse have some application both in friendly and in hostile relations, in peace and in war, even though some are pronouncedly more persuasive while others are pronouncedly more coercive.

The division-lines between domestic and foreign affairs are becoming increasingly blurred, and international relations can be profoundly affected by what, in form, are purely domestic matters, such as economic policies which, if undertaken by a Great Power, can undermine the trade or currency of the smaller Powers dependent upon it. It is not, however, unrealistic to concentrate on the forms of direct state interaction for the simple reason that any domestic matter with a sufficiently strong international component is bound to be taken up internationally without much delay.

The various instruments and techniques will be analysed according to the fields within which they operate. A large proportion of state behaviour is verbal and falls within two categories known as diplomacy and propaganda. The fields of economics and of military activities show specific characteristics and, according to tradition, are treated separately.

Diplomacy

The word 'diplomacy' is often employed in a broad meaning which embraces both the making and the execution of foreign policy. In its more technical meaning here employed it has been aptly described by George F. Kennan, the prominent American practitioner and scholar, as 'the business of communicating between governments'.

Diplomacy is the inevitable outcome of the co-existence of separate political units with any degree of contact and, indeed, its origins can be traced to remote antiquity. Greece, Byzantium, and Renaissance Italy made notable contributions to the evolution of contemporary diplomacy. At all times rulers considered diplomacy an important instrument of state policies but gradually it transcended a purely national role. Although the diplomats were governed exclusively by the dictates of national policy and ruthlessly employed cunning, deceit, and duplicity, as realistically described by Machiavelli in *The Prince*, they slowly evolved a certain orderliness of procedure. In the eighteenth century the common interest in the maintenance of an international equilibrium led to a fundamental reorganization. The balance of power system, which will be discussed in the following chapter, demanded constant vigilance from its participants and hence diplomatic missions became permanent instead of sporadic. This, in turn, led to the consolidation of diplomatic procedures and practices which was facilitated by the common aristocratic origin of the practitioners and by the common interest in the existing international order; in 1815, after the end of the Napoleonic Wars, the process was formalized by the regulations of Aix-la-Chapelle.

Thus the interest of all states in international order transformed the nature of diplomacy. Since the national interests of the several states could not be successfully secured except through the maintenance of the balance of power, diplomacy had to serve the requirements of the system as a whole. Instead of the intrigues and deceit prevalent earlier in history, the qualities of integrity, good faith, and honest negotiation became increasingly stressed. While remaining a major instrument of state policy, diplomacy became also a major agency operating on behalf of international society.

The golden age of diplomacy passed together with the balance of power system and, following the fundamental changes in international society since 1918, we entered an era of what is often called popular or new diplomacy. One fundamental reason for this was the transformation of technology and communications. Already in 1919 the actual heads of the governments of the Allied and Associated Powers spent long periods together, deliberating over the Peace Treaty with Germany. Since then, the evolution of aeroplanes and of radio has greatly increased the speed of diplomacy and therefore has reduced the importance of the diplomats in the field; to a large extent diplomacy now overlaps with policy-making. Moreover, mass-communications have opened the means of direct approach to the people of other countries through propaganda, and this not only detracts from the importance of diplomacy but sometimes conflicts with its basic purposes as well as its day-to-day operation.

Moreover, in the West, public opinion has forcibly intruded into the conduct of foreign policy and has weakened the esteem in which diplomacy was formerly held. The people were suspicious of power politics and of the balance of power system which had led to the 1914–18 War; hence they suspended diplomacy as the main instrument of foreign policy and attacked its traditional secrecy. President Wilson, the most influential spokesman of the new view, formulated the ideal in the very first of his famous Fourteen Points:

Open convenants of peace, openly arrived at, after which there shall be no private international understandings of any kind, but diplomacy shall proceed always frankly and in the public view.

Open diplomacy means two things—first, that there should be no secret agreements; second, that negotiations should be in the open. While the former condition is reasonable and is firmly rooted in democratic theory, the latter has proved embarrassing. Once the diplomats state their national demands in public, they generally cannot agree to a compromise without loss of face; in other words, they cannot negotiate.

Third, the composition of international society has now completely changed. Europe is no longer the exclusive centre of international affairs and, since the last war, power has become concentrated in the hands of two non-European states, the United States and the Soviet Union. The numbers of the members of international society are swelling with the emancipation of colonial territories in Asia and in Africa; the new states are even more remote from European diplomatic traditions than the two Superpowers.

Moreover, the United Nations has become an important supplementary and, to some extent, a competitive channel for international intercourse, some of which is conducted in the traditional manner by the diplomatic representatives to the United Nations whose private negotiations are particularly useful to states which do not maintain direct diplomatic relations. However, the United Nations also represents a new dimension in diplomacy, sometimes called diplomacy by conference, or by parliamentary procedures, or forensic diplomacy. This diplomacy is conducted openly in conferences or assemblies, and instead of the art of compromise it requires the art of persuasion, to secure the votes of as many members as possible. Since the egalitarian nature of international organization generally ensures one vote for each state, the wooing of many becomes essential.

Finally, instead of operating within a fairly stable international society based upon the operation of a balance of power in which all the members were interested, diplomacy today operates in a world in which the rival blocs are rent by ideological rifts and have little community of interest. While the new states are interested mainly in economic growth and in preserving their newly won independence from entanglement in the cold war, the communist and the Western blocs suspect each other of aggressive designs. Although it is logically arguable that both share a vital interest in the continuation of the present balance of terror and in the prevention of the spread of nuclear weapons which could upset this balance, the implications of this common interest have not as yet been absorbed by diplomacy.

The organization of diplomatic machinery has remained unaltered ever since the beginning of the nineteenth century but, owing to the multiplication of state units, only the Superpowers can maintain separate diplomatic relations with most of them. Provided no difficulties of recognition arise, most states exchange diplomatic missions only with the Superpowers, with neighbours, and with other states with which they have much business. These missions are either embassies headed by ambassadors or, less frequently and on a lower ceremonial level, legations headed by ministers. Whereas in the nineteenth century ambassadorial status was granted less frequently, only to important Powers, nowadays it has become more a mark of good relations and an expression of goodwill. The chief functions of diplomacy remain the protection of the interests of the country and of its citizens abroad, representation (legal, symbolic, and social), observation, and reporting, and, most importantly, negotiation.

Negotiations cover an extremely wide range of international transactions and can be conducted in various ways—by the ambassador of a country in the capital of another, or by its foreign ministry in its own capital; heads of government or foreign ministers engage in 'summit diplomacy' or use their personal agents; diplomatic representatives accredited to the United Nations or to a third country may be in charge, especially if the two countries have no direct diplomatic relations; special international conferences may be convened. Negotiations may be formal, conducted through an exchange of notes, or informal, through personal, sometimes unofficial contacts. The basic objective of all negotiations is to obtain from other states consent to what is considered to be in the national interest—it may be an agreement on limitation of armaments, or support in the General Assembly of the United Nations, or the conclusion of a trade agreement, or protection of the interests of nationals living in the other state, or anything else which may be quite vital or merely trivial. Negotiations necessarily begin with an exchange of statements of the views of both parties and consist essentially of bargaining, of seeking a compromise between these views. Areas of mutual agreement are defined and as far as possible enlarged, areas of disagreement are defined and as far as possible reduced through mutual compromise until accord is reached. This may be entirely informal or it may be embodied in a formal international treaty.

When the parties are basically antagonistic, negotiations are conducted not with the usual purpose of securing agreement but to damage the position of an opponent and to express hostility. It happened in the past, for instance, when the Chinese were negotiating with Lord Napier at Canton in 1830 or when the Russian bolsheviks met the Germans at Brest Litovsk in 1919; it is happening frequently today under the impact of the cold war. In spite of their avowed desire to negotiate, the communists and often also the Americans appear to be intractable; possibly during the prolonged negotiations on disarmament neither side ever seriously contemplated or desired a compromise.

Public announcements and behind-the-scene negotiations do not always coincide. When the Russians and then the Americans resumed nuclear testing in 1962, they accused each other in public of committing crimes against humanity. But, because they wished to prevent other Powers from developing nuclear weapons, these public condemnations did not prevent them from privately seeking an agreement to ban tests, though not before they had completed a further series. Such divergence between public announcements and private behaviour may appear cynical but in fact the two Powers quite reasonably combined vital national interests with propaganda warfare.

In all negotiating it is imperative to save face. For instance, in the Cuban crisis in 1962 President Kennedy forced Mr. Khrushchev to withdraw his missiles and bomber-planes from Cuba but enabled him to cover up his retreat by undertaking not to invade Cuba. Failing such a face-saving formula Mr. Khrushchev might have found a withdrawal impossible.

Normally negotiations are the simplest way for reconciling competing national interests and hence they perform a central function not only in the conduct of the foreign policy of every single state but also in the operation of the international system as a whole. They are invaluable in that they offer the simplest method of peaceful settlement of conflicts; as long as they are continued, the outbreak of violence is less likely. As a rule negotiations deal with concrete issues and details, and parties

concentrating on these are diverted from intractable fundamentals with the prejudices and passions involved.

The basic technique of negotiations is persuasion and compromise. Most issues, however controversial, involve a certain
community of interests; when relations between the negotiating
parties are fundamentally friendly, persuasion and compromise
often suffice. If necessary, inducements have to be offered, either
positive, such as military or technical assistance, or negative, such
as threats of unpleasant actions, in extreme cases including the
threat of force. Different states have developed different national
traditions in diplomatic style, and the discrepancies between the
communist, especially the Chinese, and the traditional Western
styles, greatly impede diplomacy today.

When mutual attitudes are diffident or hostile and the formulation of an issue or the form of compromise are difficult to reach,
sometimes a third party plays a part. It may offer its 'good offices',
and bring the two parties together; it may take part in actual
negotiations, which is called 'mediation'; it may even participate
in the determination of the terms of settlement, which is called
'conciliation'. 'Arbitration' which means a binding adjudication
by impartial arbiters, was spectacularly successful in the *Alabama*
case between Britain and the United States in 1872, and although
it did not rise to the sanguine expectations of its supporters, it is
still a potentially significant adjunct to diplomacy. In 1920 a
permanent World Court in The Hague was established to further
facilitate adjudication.

When successful, negotiations often lead to the conclusion of a
formal treaty. The significance of treaties greatly varies, depending upon their subject-matter and the identity of the parties;
most important are agreements which lay the foundation for
future co-operation on vital matters, such as alliances which are a
traditional method of pooling together the power of states with a
common political purpose and a common potential enemy. The
two important features of alliances are that they can be concluded by states as different as the Western Powers and the Soviet
Union during the last war, and that their duration fully depends
on the existence of the common enemy.

More permanent are alignments resulting from membership of
the international institutions. Normally the treaties concerned
provide some method for the termination of the institution or the

withdrawal of individual members, but the contemporary tendency is to omit such provisions. The United Nations Charter does not mention them although discussions before the signature of the treaty confirmed that withdrawal remains open; the European Economic Community is meant to be permanent.

Propaganda

By propaganda we generally understand any systematic attempt to affect the minds, emotions, and actions of a given group for a specific public purpose. While propaganda, like diplomacy, is on the whole verbal, it differs from diplomacy in two important respects. First, it is addressed to the *people* of other states rather than to their *governments* (the important subject of propaganda conducted by the government at home need not concern us here); the effect on other governments is rarely more than incidental.

Second, propaganda is selfish, governed exclusively by the national interests of the propagandist and therefore usually unacceptable to other states. There is here no attempt to find a compromise between competing national interests; the aim is exclusively the national advantage of the propagandist. As far as international order is concerned, propaganda as it is conducted by the various states serves purely negative purposes. Not only is it never employed for the purposes of this order as diplomacy occasionally is, but all international efforts to curb at least its most vicious forms have as yet been unavailing.

At the same time the division-lines between diplomacy and propaganda are not fully clear-cut. Negotiations sometimes degenerate into exercises in propaganda directed to the public and not to the governments. The Russian and the Chinese communists are cultivating extensive relations with foreign groups sympathetic to their ideology. The most important of these are the communist parties, but there are also numerous other groups often called cover-organizations, such as the national units of the World Peace Council, the World Federation of Trade Unions, the World Federation of Democratic Youth, etc. While all these serve the purposes of communist propaganda, relations with them are conducted on a quasi-diplomatic, although not governmental level.

Propaganda did not play a significant role in international affairs until the 1914–18 War. Previously only the Catholic Church had used it and had institutionalized the propagation of faith through a special Sacred Congregation (*de propaganda fide*) from the title of which the word 'propaganda' is derived. The British Government during the First World War was the first to organize and systematize the use of propaganda at home and abroad. British efforts abroad were fairly successful in securing the goodwill of the neutrals, especially the Americans, but less so in appealing to the Germans. Other belligerents did not employ propaganda quite as systematically or extensively and the organizations built up during the war disappeared after it ended.

The real impetus to the development of propaganda was given by the growth of the totalitarian countries in the inter-war period. First the Communists and then the Nazis built up tremendous and costly propaganda machineries and the western democracies were gradually forced to match their efforts. Despite the defeat of Nazism, post-war propaganda has further increased in scope. The Russians try to stir up discontent and to secure the allegiance of the people in the West while the Americans have parallel aims regarding the people of the communist bloc. Even more important are the competing appeals to the peoples and also the governments of the uncommitted countries. Agencies which are in charge of these propaganda activities, the United States Information Agency and the Agitation and Propaganda Section of the Central Committee of the Soviet Communist Party, have assumed considerable importance and operate on large annual budgets. Here, as in the field of armaments, other states find it difficult to compete. For instance, British propaganda (officially referred to as information services), although relatively cheap and highly successful, has been chronically suffering from the lack of adequate and assured finance. It remains decentralized and is conducted by the Central Office of Information, by the Overseas Services of the B.B.C., and also by the British Council.

Among the varied instruments of propaganda, short-wave radio is by far the most important since broadcasts can reach audiences anywhere in the world and cannot be 100 per cent effectively blocked. Hence much of the money spent on propaganda goes into radio transmitters and programmes and, in communist states, also into transmitters which interfere with foreign broadcasts. While this interference is not fully successful, governments can much more easily prevent the distribution of propaganda materials in printed form and have full control over personal travel.

In all propaganda activities the first problem is how to reach physically the people at whom it is directed; it is largely technological and its successful solution depends on sufficient resources and skill. When the target can be reached, there arise difficult psychological problems which are similar to those of commercial advertising: how to capture the attention of the people and how to achieve the desired response. These determine the method of presentation.

A simple way to conduct propaganda is to present news and information as objectively and factually as possible and to leave the listener or reader to reach his own conclusions. A straight-out information service can be politically effective, especially when it reaches totalitarian societies which try to limit their citizens to sources of information suitably vetted by the government. It has the great advantage of attracting attention since the listeners or readers will be generally interested in correcting the distorted and suspect picture presented at home. Complete objectivity is, of course, scarcely realizable and, even in the most factual and dispassionate services, a selection from the various items competing for attention is generally made to emphasize favourable rather than disparaging news. The B.B.C. earned a justified reputation for concern with truth during the Second World War and since and, in order to retain the interest and the trust of its listeners, it must constantly guard against deviating too far from its high standards of objectivity. Nevertheless, in presenting news to overseas listeners, the B.B.C. could scarcely be expected to stress the backwardness of the British shipbuilding industry as much as the up-to-date character of electronics or aviation, or the relative inadequacy of old-age pensions rather than the advanced nature of the National Health Service.

The opposite technique is that of the 'Big Lie'. It was effectively used by Hitler who acted according to his argument developed in *Mein Kampf*, that a lie, provided it is sufficiently big and is frequently repeated, will be at least partly believed by the masses; most people lack the imagination to conceive that repeated statements are not all true. The censorship of alternative sources of information is essential for this technique to be effective. Falsehood on a minor scale is much less useful and can undermine trust in the sources of information. Hence the United States calls its information activities since the war a 'strategy of truth' and, without quite achieving it, tries to earn the reputation of objectivity enjoyed by the B.B.C.

The form of the news must be reasonably attractive in order to gain attention. The public are not interested in ponderous analyses of the rights and wrongs of any issue but readily respond to simple slogans, however loosely related to it, provided they contain such emotionally valuable words as peace, aggression, human rights, self-determination, etc. Visual impressions and physical demonstrations add greatly to the influence of propaganda. Nuclear explosions and launchings of satellites now supplement the age-long tradition of military parades and of naval demonstrations. Visits by prominent politicians, leaders and artists, even travel by the man in the street, all play a part in drawing attention to the propagandist state.

Not only attention but also response is required, and the propagandist must establish a degree of rapport between himself and his targets by appealing to their own local interests, experiences and outlook. Hence propagandists tend to stress common characteristics and interests—the Japanese spoke of the 'co-prosperity sphere', the Nazis of the Aryan race, the Russians of the solidarity of the oppressed and under-developed countries, the Chinese of the 'true' revolutionaries. Where such solidarity is not effectively established, propaganda fails, as shown by the futility of American appeals to anti-communist sentiments which are not fully shared by others. The influence of propaganda greatly increases through its frequency and consistency over a long period of time and also through the elimination or obstruction of competing sources of information.

Economics

Economic instruments differ from diplomacy and propaganda in that they are not necessarily directly operated by governments. Indeed, in the nineteenth century, international trade which was dominated by the City of London gave the appearance of being divorced from politics and completely autonomous, although as E. H. Carr has forcibly pointed out in *The Twenty Years' Crisis*, this illusion was due only to Britain's unchallenged naval supremacy. In the twentieth century, the close connection between international politics and economics has been re-established. Private interests are still paramount in the international trade of western Powers, but clearly under close governmental direction. In communist and largely also in new, under-developed countries, trade is conducted by governmental agencies.

The other characteristic peculiar to economic instruments is their great advance towards internationalization. As soon as the governments had assumed economic powers, they began to yield them to international institutions. Western trade is circumscribed by the provisions of the General Agreement on Trade and Tariffs (GATT), manipulation of exchange rates of national currencies by the membership of the International Fund; members of the European Economic Community and of its eastern counterpart, the COMECON, have surrendered much of their economic sovereignty to these organizations. There are two reasons why the economic instruments are being internationalized in advance of others. First, considerable economic advantages are secured. Second, although the close connection between economics and politics is now fully appreciated, the direct and immediate impact of economic internationalization on state sovereignty is considerably less than would be the impact of internationalization of such politically sensitive elements as armaments. Anyway, for the time being, while the most important economic institutions include only western states, the problems arising from their existence have not been politically grave.

Economic instruments are widely employed both in peace and war; in peacetime international trade and assistance are most important, in wartime and during the cold war various measures of economic warfare is employed.

To some extent all countries must engage in international trade in order to obtain some goods which they cannot produce at home, and to sell others with the proceeds of which they can pay for their imports. Beyond this indispensable minimum, international trade provides the benefits of an international division of labour under which the various goods can be obtained from the most efficient and therefore cheapest producer. Free trade, which was actively pursued by Britain between 1846 and 1932, meant to the British an economically most efficient world-wide arrangement. To other countries it meant a perpetuation of a situation in which they had little chance of developing their own industries in open competition with the established, more efficient British exporters.

Protective tariffs, the most important instrument for controlling international trade, thus arose mainly for economic reasons, to shelter budding domestic industries from foreign competition. These industries, however, were desired not only for economic welfare but also for general political purpose, as an element of state power. The Great Depression, which began in 1929, brought in its train an enormous increase in protective tariffs and also in other devices to keep out imports, such as quantitative controls (quotas) and currency restrictions.

Apart from this protective role, tariffs serve to secure better terms of trade through reciprocal arrangements but they can be used also for more clearly political purposes, as bargaining weapons in negotiations and as instruments of retaliation. Here the element of size and of relative importance in the foreign trade of the country concerned is decisive. The main buyers of a country's produce or the main suppliers of its vital imports are obviously influential. The Southern States used their position as the major suppliers of cotton for the Lancashire industry in their endeavour to secure British support during the American Civil War; the Austrians were able to bring Serbia to heel through declining to buy her pigs during the so-called 'Pig War' in 1905; Britain exercised a similar pressure on Ireland through the 'tariff war' of 1932–36; Hitler dominated Eastern Europe in the late thirties by offering the only available large-scale market for its agricultural exports—he enjoyed a position which approached monopoly.

Through a deliberate policy, international trade can be directed within a group of states to enhance its economy but also to reinforce its political coherence, for instance in the various colonial systems, or in the communist bloc, and in the European Economic Community today.

The present trend towards the liberalization of international trade and the establishment of international economic institutions have greatly reduced the freedom of the states to control their trade individually. Within the blocs, individual control is being superseded by an institutionalized co-operation; inter-bloc trade can be more suitably discussed under the heading of economic warfare.

For a long time investment in foreign countries was private and for economic purposes. It has continued to be so from the time of the great banking houses of the Fuggers in the sixteenth century, or the Rothschilds after the Napoleonic Wars, to the industrial empires and the great oil companies of our own generation. These investments were not divorced from politics, and the national governments encouraged or discouraged them to suit their political aims, but the usual form of direct governmental intervention is assistance and not investment. In all periods economically weak allies had to be buttressed by military supplies and political loans or grants, but since the last war grants have surpassed all precedents. By the colossal expenditure of over 20,000 million dollars, especially through the Marshall Plan, the Americans have helped to restore the economies and to modernize the armed forces of Western Europe. They have been dispensing money for military support and for economic aid also outside Europe; the funds are continuing to flow out at a diminishing but still substantial rate. In the mid-fifties the Russians began to offer large-scale economic assistance, and their competition with the Americans has become an important feature of the cold war. Sometimes the Superpowers court the same governments, for instance those in India, in Afghanistan, or in Egypt. More often they support governments inclined more to them: thus the Americans have been helping the Philippines, South Korea, South Vietnam, and Jaiwan while the Russians have been supporting the Fidel Castro government of Cuba. All the colonial Powers, especially France and Britain, have given considerable assistance to their colonies and ex-colonies.

Even in peacetime the unfriendly purpose of economic policies can justify their classification as economic warfare. Such is the boycott of trade which is usually conducted by the people rather than the government, but which may have governmental support —one example is the Chinese boycott of British and Japanese goods in the inter-war period. Or it may be an action against the currency of another state, as in London in 1923 when the French occupied the Ruhr against the wishes of the British.

A state may resort to 'dumping' in order to dislocate production and the world markets—thus in 1958 the Soviet Union resold, with disruptive results, quantities of Chinese tin at a price below that paid to the Chinese. Economic warfare can take also the form of the closing and opening of markets. In 1960, when the Americans became convinced of the hostility of the Castro Government in Cuba, they gradually brought to a halt the imports of Cuban sugar which had enjoyed a privileged market in their country; as a counter-move in economic warfare, in order to stabilize a regime hostile to the United States, the communist bloc stepped in and offered new markets for this sugar.

In wartime a belligerent may resort to 'pre-emption' of vital strategic materials from neutrals in order to deny them to the adversary, as the British tried to do in the last war with Spanish copper and Turkish chrome.

The best-established war-measure is naval blockade. Britain has been employing it ever since the times of Elizabeth I, it played an important part in the Napoleonic and the two World Wars, and is still by no means obsolete. The effectiveness of economic measures gave rise to the idea of 'economic sanctions' which were embodied in the League of Nations Covenant as a promising expedient for curbing aggression without military intervention. The League applied such sanctions only once, against Italy in 1935 for her aggression against Ethiopia. The sanctions failed but probably only because the members were half-hearted in their support. In 1951 the United Nations decided in favour of economic sanctions against Communist China, in 1962 it was moving towards such sanctions against Katanga, and, in 1963, against South Africa. It employed them again ineffectively against Southern Rhodesia.

The cold war has led to many measures which can be called economic warfare. Each bloc tries to deprive its opponent of the supplies of strategically important materials and products. Communist international trade is rigidly controlled, and the Americans have been making strenuous but not fully successful attempts to curb Western exports of 'strategic' materials to the communist bloc.

Military Power and War

In contrast to economics, the military field has been fully monopolized by governments. Only a few individuals and groups possess weapons independently of governmental control, and these are quite insignificant in international relations unless they stage a successful rebellion. Nevertheless, the states are strongly circumscribed by international considerations. A unilateral military strategy would be possible only for a state sufficiently powerful to be able to cope with its rivals by itself, or under a policy of isolationism which, as has been explained, is not feasible in the world today. Whether employing the contemporary expedient of alliances and coalitions, or participating in any scheme of collective security of the future, states are no longer in full control of the military instrument.

This instrument looms large in all considerations of foreign policy and is extremely costly, and in all states, particularly so in the Superpowers, it swallows up a large slice of the national product. Moreover, technological changes and the resulting changes in the structure and the operation of international society raise a host of questions about the usefulness of the instrument, questions which are of such fundamental nature that some of them cannot yet be adequately formulated, let alone answered.

The problem can be easily grasped from a glance at some national defence policies. In Britain, annual expenditure over the last few years has been over £2,000 million. The frequent criticisms of British defence policy arose from the two connected views that this policy has been excessively costly, to the detriment of pressing social needs, and that it has been ineffective, incapable of securing vital national interests. The second criticism is more fundamental, and opinions about cost obviously depend on the answer it receives. Particularly violent was the argument about the usefulness of nuclear weapons. While the unilateral nuclear disarmers regarded the whole expenditure on the nuclear deterrent immoral and wasteful, more moderate critics stressed the illusory character of the 'independent deterrent' and the inadequacy of the conventional armaments due partly to the diversion of funds to nuclear weapons, and partly to the inefficiencies resulting from the conservatism of military thinking and from the competition between the three traditional services, the Navy, the Army, and the Air Force.

In the United States, concentration upon nuclear weapons in the late forties has given way to a parallel effort in conventional armaments. Although the American economy can sustain both and massive aid to allies, too, the question of the future size of the defence effort and of its adequacy for ensuring the defence of the country are continuously debated. In France the expenditure on nuclear weapons will be steeply mounting in the seventies while the effectiveness of the conventional arms is likely to come under discussion since, despite her costly efforts, France has failed in her two colonial wars, in Indo-China and in Algeria, and has also withdrawn from the military organs of NATO. In the Soviet Union and in China the competition between guns and butter is stark.

In order to tackle rationally the involved problem of the military instrument, we must clarify its actual role in international relations. Many of the criticisms of military expenditure somewhat naïvely assume that such expenditure, if more efficiently managed, could ensure national security and major national interests. This assumption is untenable. We should not exaggerate the value of the military instrument; complete security is unthinkable in the nuclear era and other, non-military instruments are growing in importance, especially in dealings with the uncommitted countries.

Another source of confusion arises from the fear of another total war and from the resulting attempts to eliminate violence from international relations. Weapons can be used in two capacities—in attack, in order to secure a change, or defensively, to deter a possible attacker and rebut him if an attack actually takes place. The policy of nuclear deterrence is not a complete innovation, but merely a modern adaptation of the old Latin adage *si vis pacem para bellum*. The Second World War was a catastrophic disappointment to the naïve disarmers and supporters of disarmament and international organization who believed that violence could be eliminated from the world without an adequate supervisory force. Nevertheless, although the central role played by the military instrument is now more generally appreciated, the situation is still often obscured by unrealistically sharp distinctions between the states of war and peace and between nuclear and conventional weapons.

As has been repeatedly stressed, state interaction combines both antagonism and community of interest. This means that conflict is never fully separated from co-operation nor co-operation from conflict. Indeed, different periods of history combine the two in varying measures, and the difference between the states of peace and war lies merely in the degree to which one of these elements predominates. If negotiations are the general way in which international issues are tackled and if force is employed only marginally, we speak about peace; if violence is openly employed as the main method of settling such issues, we speak of war. This state of affairs was not altered when the Peace Treaty of Westphalia established peace as the normal mode of international relations in Europe or when international lawyers developed two separate bodies of rules of international law known as the law of peace and the law of war. The cold war, the name commonly given to the post-war period, makes clear how unreal the distinction is. The cold war is neither peace nor war; hostile relations predominate, but not to the exclusion of negotiations, and the use of violence remains circumscribed. We cannot fully explain the place of the military instrument in the cold war either in terms of peace or of war.

Despite our natural preoccupation with the prevention of war, we must not lose sight of the fact that war has been traditionally filling an important social role in international society. Whenever a state wishes to enforce a rule of law which is in its favour but is disobeyed by another state, or to alter an adverse rule, in the absence of any superior authority to deal with these matters, it must perforce resort to violence. It is difficult, if at all possible, to deprive the states of their ultimate right to wage war unless some other effective method of enforcement of law and of peaceful change is devised. Otherwise the world would be frozen without the possibility of change to conform with justice and with changing social conditions, and even existing rights could be violated with impunity. It is arguable that the General Assembly of the United Nations already acts as an agent of peaceful change although only in a limited fashion. It was instrumental in hastening colonial emancipation but is still helpless even against not particularly powerful members who refuse to comply.

The other unrealistically sharp distinction is that made between conventional and nuclear, or more broadly speaking, non-conventional weapons. The former are less destructive and better understood; their use could be left unlimited or slightly circumscribed by international law without endangering the continuation of the national states or of international order as these exist today. The latter have enormous destructive potentialities, the political implications of which cannot as yet be clearly perceived, and hence their control or, if possible, elimination is the only satisfying solution. In fact, the distinction is less clear. The devastating Second World War was fought with conventional weapons alone, while some of the 'non-conventional' weapons, such as low-yield tactical nuclear devices or mild forms of nerve-gas which only temporarily disable human beings exposed to them, are less destructive than some of the most powerful conventional weapons. The dangers of 'escalation' (a milder form of warfare gradually leading to more severe forms) is such that a rigid division-line is untenable.

The military instrument provides the background of assuredness and stability for diplomacy. 'Negotiation from strength' is a sound precept; without the backing of military power, no state can avoid concessions detrimental to its vital interests if irresistible pressures and threats are brought to bear upon it. The western Powers withstood Soviet pressures on their exposed position in Berlin, both during the Berlin Blockade in 1948 and 1949, and again after November 1958, only because they were militarily strong.

Strength alone is insufficient unless the prospective opponent is aware of it and takes it into account. Hence international relations in most ages, particularly so during the cold war, abound in references to and in demonstrations of strength. Armaments and troop formations are displayed during national day parades; naval demonstrations are staged; troops are mobilized or massed along the frontier or shifted to bases in sensitive places. A show of force is a much easier and cheaper expedient than its actual use and it may sometimes be quite effective. It is possible that the Chinese communists were eventually forced to conclude the dragging armistice negotiations on Korea only by the dispatch of American nuclear weapons to Okinawa, a show of strength implying that they might be used if necessary.

Finally, the military instrument may be actually employed. It is here that the notion of the dichotomy between war and peace constitutes a serious obstacle to understanding because the use of violence is by no means limited to war. Even the classical international law of peace permits the employment of violence which falls short of war under such names as reprisals, measures tinged with a hostile character, or pre-belligerent measures, or measures short of war.

An actual example may explain the distinction made here, and it is best chosen from relations between unfriendly countries in which the military instrument is much more prominent than in the relations between countries which are friendly. Since the Arab countries are hostile, Israel relies on the military instruments to a very large extent. She came into existence through the use of violence, as the result of the victory of the Jewish military forces in the war against the Arabs in 1947. She still relies upon this instrument for her survival, being faced, as she is, with the Arab desire to terminate her independent existence. In order to remind their neighbours of their military strength, the Israelis often parade it and occasionally use it in frontier raids (which serve also the narrower objective of warning against Arab infringements of the border). In 1956, when faced with growing danger from the Egyptians who were receiving military supplies from the communist bloc, the Israelis used their forces for a large-scale military operation in the Sinai Peninsula. They scored a victory over the Egyptian forces and greatly damaged Egyptian morale but were forced to withdraw under pressure from the United Nations. Then the Israeli military instrument reverted to its previous deterrent role and was actively used only in minor frontier skirmishes, but in a situation similar to 1956, it was again used fully in the lightning 'Six-days War' of June 1968.

It is important to note the fact that only conventional weapons have been actually used since 1945, and invariably in a somewhat restricted form. The Americans and the Russians have refrained from a direct clash and in all conflicts, at least on one side, fighting was done by proxy, by an ally. The situation shows gradations from guerilla warfare, sometimes conducted by extremely small groups, as in 1961 and 1962 in Laos, to such approximations to a major war as the conflict fought out in Korea in 1950–1 and in Vietnam since 1966. Armed forces were used extensively also outside the context of the cold war, particularly in numerous colonial struggles.

In the policy of deterrence nuclear weapons have served only as a general background for diplomacy and have not been actually employed. The fundamental principle of this complex policy is simple. The weapons are stored not in order to strike but in order to inspire the opponent with the conviction that they would be automatically employed following any serious attack by him. As long as this policy is successful, the nuclear weapons will not be actually used. Since deterrence is rightly considered as fundamentally important, both sides resort to frequent reminders and demonstrations of their nuclear power; the launchings of satellites and nuclear tests serve this, as well as purely technological ends. Moreover, the Americans, at least, have been devoting much thought to making their deterrent credible, to ensuring that the Russians would be in no doubt as to whether the weapons would be actually used, if necessary.

It may be added that there is little justification for equating the existence of nuclear weapons with the danger of an all-out nuclear war. Admittedly, the ingenious American doctrine of 'graduated deterrence', based upon the possibility of nuclear conflicts limited in scope, do not sound very convincing. The argument is that even if nuclear weapons were employed in any future conflict, neither side is likely to resort to an all-out attack on the opponent's cities, which would provoke immediate retaliation; hence a war would be fought by small-scale, tactical nuclear weapons alone, or be limited to an attack on the opponent's 'counterforce'. Such limitations are not very credible however, owing to the dangers of escalation; the side suffering a disadvantage at any level would be sorely tempted to proceed to the next in order to recoup its fortunes, until an all-out war is eventually reached.

Deterrence, or the nuclear balance of power, provides a basis for a certain degree of stability of the present international order, and we have not as yet found any possible substitute. The basis of stability is, however, brittle. It may be destroyed by the proliferation of nuclear weapons or by a technological breakthrough, e.g. in anti-ballistic missiles and by a consequent armaments race. Moreover, deterrence serves mainly conservative aims, to preserve the *status quo*. It does circumscribe revisionist policies by eliminating the likelihood of an immediate all-out nuclear war which would be pernicious to all, but if the limited struggles do not succeed, escalation may eventually lead to it.

So far, war and the use of force have been discussed only as techniques of foreign policy. Their place in international relations can be more fully explained only within the context of international order.

6

International Society and its Current Problems

The Nature of International Order

SOCIETY OR COMMUNITY, system or order, are the several terms used to describe the international environment. It is unnecessary for our purpose to draw precise distinctions between these terms, which are used sometimes interchangeably but often distinctively, although, even in the latter case, they overlap. There is no full agreement on terminology but little disagreement about the fundamental nature of the reality—that it consists of a number of units which interact. It is clear that these units conduct their relations not in a social vacuum but within a broader system which evolves its own structure, norms, and rules of behaviour.

International systems lack the two prerequisites of domestic political systems—the social basis of a community and the political structure of a government. Instead of an unconditional agreement on co-operation, on the precedence of common good over sub-group or individual interests, international systems can build only upon a limited and conditional co-operation which sometimes degenerates into complete chaos. They completely lack a hierarchically arranged government which determines the jurisdiction of all the social sub-groups, and has the means to enforce its norms of law. The meaning of sovereignty is quite different in both contexts. While internal sovereignty means that the government is supreme within the political system of the state, that the whole takes precedence over the parts, external sovereignty means that the governments are supreme within the international system, that the parts take precedence over the whole. In other words, while within the states political systems are strongly centralized, international systems are strongly decentralized.

Nevertheless, as the terminology employed indicates, international systems do not entirely lack structure and sets of norms which regulate the behaviour of their members, although these structures are invariably much looser and the sets of norms much weaker than those distinguishable within states. The interplay among the units and between them and the international order as a whole is affected by the nature of each historical system. Hence an analysis of the nature of the system operating in a given time and place is essential for the understanding of international relations taking place within it. The study of the behaviour of single states, or of states in mutual interaction, is insufficient in itself.

It is possible to analyse international systems in an abstract theoretical manner, discussing 'ideal types'. For instance, allowing for the fact that most systems fall somewhere in between, we can distinguish two extreme types, one which is completely dominated by the units and the other by the central institutions of the system. It is also possible to concentrate on historical international systems, particularly modern ones. We shall try to combine both approaches. While it is obviously important to study the balance of power system which was operating from 1648 to 1914, since it has been the basis of contemporary international society and the source of our terminology, it would be difficult, if at all possible, to specify the causes for its disintegration and to estimate the significance of subsequent changes without some theoretical appraisal. By necessity we must break up the chronological flow of events into tidy units, periodize and systematize, and it is preferable that we undertake this operation consciously, explicitly stating the underlying theory.

The main topic of this book being the interaction among states, and the main contemporary issue being the avoidance of war, we may seek the criteria for periodization in a combination of three inter-related elements for which Professor Stanley Hoffmann has suggested the name *stakes of conflict*. First, there is the fundamental question of the identity of the units, a question the importance of which can be seen in the transition from the Roman Empire to the medieval system, or from the nineteenth-century system of multi-national and colonial empires to the present. Then, there is the question of technology, a fundamental change in which, like the invention of gunpowder or of nuclear energy, completely alters the scope of possible actions. Finally, there is the question of what the units want to do to one another, whether they are prepared to co-operate within the existing order or whether some of them attempt to revise it. Attitudes to the existing order are conditioned by the environment, both international and domestic, but influence this order in turn. It is impossible to determine to what extent changes in human ideas, attitudes and desires are the cause or the effect of changed circumstances. Undoubtedly there is a certain amount of circularity, and a fundamental change in any of these elements is likely to lead to a fundamental change in others.

A distinction should be made between stable international systems in which the three elements fluctuate only moderately, and others in which changes are so violent that they become revolutionary. The reasons for and the implications of the relative stability of the international system preceding the First World War offer a promising approach to the understanding of the revolutionary character of the contemporary system.

The Balance of Power System

The expression 'balance of power' is used to describe a tendency towards an equilibrium which some writers discern in international relations as well as in many social and physical domains; it denotes also state politics aiming at such an equilibrium. Here it is used strictly as a name for the international system between 1648 and 1914. By present standards, this system lasted over a long period of nearly three centuries and showed remarkable stability in surviving the challenge of the French Revolution and the Napoleonic Wars. Some of the most pertinent questions to be asked are those about the nature of this challenge and the way in which it was met.

There are good reasons for regarding the balance of power as an important innovation in the history of mankind. For the first time since the destruction of the Roman Empire, Europe achieved a fair degree of stability; moreover, it was a stability not of the unacceptable hegemonial type, based on conquest and

domination by a single Power. In conformity with modern ideas
and with the forces of nationalism, the new system was plural; it
embraced several Great Powers and it gradually transcended the
boundaries of Europe. Also, for the first time in the modern
period of history, all the participants accepted that the system was
important for them. This did not mean that considerations of
international order generally prevailed over the selfishness of
states, that a community-feeling transcending single states became
strong. On the contrary, states remained as competitive and suspicious as ever, each continuing as the supreme arbiter of its behaviour, ultimately free to break the rules of the system. As in
all previous systems, this selfishness could and actually did lead to
attempts by states with sufficiently promising power to conquer
others and to upset the system.

Simultaneously, however, the balance of power was a much
more articulated, thought-out system than any of its predecessors.
If the member states were not invariably ready to accept the
norms it was imposing upon them, they were conscious at least of
their common advantage in protecting those norms from being
violated by others. When a state made a bid for power, other
states tended to join forces in defence; the major challenge of
Louis XIV, or Napoleon, or the Kaiser, all eventually ended in
defeat at the hands of opposing coalitions.

Stability was based upon the balanced redistribution of territory by the Peace Treaty of Westphalia which established several
major states capable of maintaining an equilibrium of power
among themselves. Legitimacy was the foundation of the post-
Napoleonic settlement and no major changes in units ensued.
During the nineteenth century the Ottoman Empire gradually
disintegrated, but this Empire had never been essential for the
system, and the event was merely a harbinger for the disintegration of multi-national empires during and after the 1914–18 War.
Order was more seriously disturbed when powerful new units
arose through the unification of Italy and Germany.

Although all states, large and small, powerful and weak, were
participating, theoretically on the basis of sovereign equality, in
fact the balance was maintained only by the few powerful states;
it was a balance of power among the Great Powers, and the
system depended on their co-existence. Fortunately there were
several such Powers, as five is the minimum number facilitating a

steady equilibrium. Two Great Powers would almost certainly end in a headlong clash, while four would tend to form two rigid combinations of two states each, which could be altered only by an extremely dangerous reversal of alliances. Like triumvirate governments, balance of power based upon three units would be inherently unstable since a state would have little opportunity for re-alignment and therefore would have a strong incentive for striking first; the only possible regrouping following a war would be an obviously risky and therefore unlikely combination of the weaker of the victorious Powers with the defeated Power. Thus it was for the benefit of the system that there were so many Great Powers.

Stability was increased by several favourable circumstances. There were no dramatic technological changes similar to the invention of nuclear weapons; there was plenty of room for economic development; overseas expansion was a useful safety-valve which enabled the states to increase their power without seriously endangering rivals, and offered wide scope in the game of compensations, necessary to maintain the balance. Industrialization and colonial expansion were much more promising means of augmenting state-power than the subjugation of another European state. Territorial expansion in Europe was impeded not only by other members of the system who were apprehensive that the equilibrium might be destroyed but also by communications which remained very poor until the end of the nineteenth century, and by the growing influence of nationalism. Thus Bismarck would have found it very difficult to occupy France for any length of time after the Prussian victories in 1870–1.

The system was based on the continuation of the traditional pursuit of security by each unit through its individual efforts, but it offered opportunities for negotiations instead of fighting, and for the conclusion of temporary alliances to counterbalance the power of others. When challenges to the equilibrium could not be staved off in a peaceful way, wars did break out but they were not fought to eliminate the opponent. Restraint in victory was not due to altruistic reasons but to a realistic concern with the system, to preserve the vanquished state as a potential future ally.

Domestic pressures became less cogent. Religion lost its fanatical appeal, mercantilism and absolutism gradually weakened

within the Great Powers. The rulers and diplomats of all countries were conscious of their 'corporate identity' and agreed upon
the legitimacy of the balance. Hence they found no reason to
interfere with powerful trans-national links, the intellectual links
based on the Enlightenment and the commercial links of international trade. Tolerance at home and abroad extended to the
domestic systems of other states. Since full flexibility of the balance of power demanded that states should be completely independent, the lawyers perfected the theories of state sovereignty, of
impenetrability of territory, and of non-intervention.

Only the more powerful states were necessary for the maintenance of the system, but the theories of sovereignty were extended to lesser Powers, too, first in Europe, then in Latin
America, and subsequently throughout the world. These smaller
states were admitted on the basis of 'sovereign equality', but their
role in the system was mainly passive. They were not so much
potential allies who could make an impact on the power of
alliances, as potential areas of expansion for the Great Powers
who could, through conquering them, become dominant. Though
in themselves the smaller states were not essential for the working
of the system, their elimination presented problems too difficult
to be worth while. Within the framework of flexible alliances the
Great Powers could not agree upon any workable division of
Europe and they usually preferred to make use of the much more
profitable and politically less dangerous opportunities for expansion outside Europe. Only one smaller state was divided, and the
experience was scarcely encouraging. Russia, Prussia, and Austria
carved up Poland rather gingerly in three consecutive partitions
towards the end of the eighteenth century, but the Polish question remained one of the most explosive topics of international
politics. The incorporation of dissatisfied Poles who occasionally
rose in arms scarcely enhanced the power of the occupants. They
managed to maintain an equilibrium in eastern Europe but
probably could have done so more efficiently had Poland been
left independent.

The system was severely challenged by the French Revolution.
In the first place, the Revolution introduced changes at home,
with a new regime which assumed full and intolerant governmental control over the citizens and prepared the path for Napoleon with his exorbitant ambitions. Internationally, the Revolu-

tion destroyed the solidarity of a homogeneous Europe through its ideas, and the balance of power through its victories; as the result of the Napoleonic Wars all frontiers became unstable and Europe was rent by ideological and national antagonisms of a very serious nature. The victors decided in favour of legitimacy, of the restoration of the pre-war system in preference to the accommodation of the new forces. The balance was restored and so was France as one of its essential units, under her previous Bourbon rulers and within her pre-revolutionary boundaries.

Between 1815 and 1914 the system evolved the Concert of Europe. Britain rejected the Russian proposal for the much further-reaching Holy Alliance, a loose world government to be worked jointly by the Great Powers, with the right to intervene in the domestic affairs of other states. The Concert was merely a loose consultative institution which refrained from intervention in the domestic affairs of states. It permitted many small wars, but prevented these wars from becoming general and upsetting the balance of power. Nineteenth-century Europe neatly balanced conservation and change, and can be credited with many positive achievements. The behaviour of the Great Powers was, on the whole, moderate, as epitomized in the lenient peace concluded by Bismarck with Austria after her crushing defeat at Sadowa. There was general stability and no states disappeared, but such major political changes as the emancipation of the Balkan people from Ottoman rule and the neutralization of Switzerland, Belgium, and Luxembourg were achieved with little violence; international law developed and, towards the end of the century, colonial expansion came under a degree of internationally agreed regulation. It must, however, be borne in mind that these achievements cannot be credited to the balance of power and the Concert of Europe alone since they were made possible by exceptionally favourable conditions for the economic and political expansion of the system.

In the latter part of the century conditions began to deteriorate, as did also the attitude of Germany, one of the five Great Powers. The process of colonial expansion ground itself to a halt when there were no further lands available for occupation, and economic expansion degenerated into competition among rival national economies; in contrast to his great lenience to Austria, which had been defeated only four years earlier, Bismarck severed

Alsace-Lorraine from France after the 1870–1 War. This led to a continuing French grievance, and deprived the international system of a large proportion of its flexibility; from 1871 France was permanently aligned against Germany. Instead of working through fluctuating alliances, the system broke up into two opposing camps; slowly but gradually the diplomatic fronts hardened and eventually clashed in August, 1914.

The Search for a New Order

Balance of power being the only known modern form of international order, it dominated political thought and activities in the first half of the twentieth century. Attitudes to it varied. Some thinkers considered it as the only possible promise of peace, others rejected it as being responsible for the First World War, but whether endeavouring to improve the working of the system or to replace it by something new, they were all thinking in terms of the nineteenth-century experience and were employing the concepts inherited from it.

The system slowly changed from a European to a global one. Around the break of the century two non-European states, the United States and Japan, were admitted to the status of Great Powers, but as their participation did not become as intimate as that of the European states, the system became looser. At the same time, through her naval challenge to Britain, Germany made a bid for the extension of the balance of power system from Europe to the oceans of the world. She confidently but vainly expected that, provided there was a sufficiently powerful German navy to form the nucleus of a naval coalition counterbalancing the British navy, other naval Powers would rally against Britain to establish an equilibrium in naval power similar to the balance of power in Europe. However, the distrust of Germany's power and intentions was such that, instead of pursuing the balance of power formula and joining the weaker side, the two great naval outsiders, the United States and Japan, preferred to align themselves with Britain.

With sporadic intervention by the United States, the Concert of Europe managed to settle several acute crises early in the century, but it gradually lost all remnants of its flexibility. In vain did Sir Edward Grey try to galvanize it into another effort in 1914, and it came to an end with the outbreak of the war in August.

The First World War was a traumatic experience for mankind. Having been lulled into a feeling of false security, people found it difficult to adjust themselves to a long war unexampled in its scope of destruction, and to contemplate the possibility of its re-currence. To many, the war meant complete bankruptcy of the old system and a challenge requiring a completely new response. They sought this response in a new type of international order, much more tightly organized. The states kept their position in it; indeed, the League of Nations Covenant guaranteed the per-petuation of their territorial integrity and political independ-ence, and the principle of national self-determination gave them a powerful moral and ideological justification. They retained also the ultimate right to resort to war in pursuit of national ends, but the League of Nations introduced a collective security system which was to replace the insecurity of fluctuating national alliances.

The inter-war world was profoundly disturbed. All the three elements determining whether a system is stable or revolutionary, pointed towards revolution. First of all, the composition of inter-national society changed. Two Great Powers, defeated Germany and communized Russia, were temporarily out of the game, many new states came into being, and Europe ceased to be the exclusive centre of world politics. With the advent of the totalitarian ideologies, first Communism, then Fascism, and finally Nazism, international society became extremely heterogeneous and some of its members intolerant and proselytizing. Second, the technological changes, the development of the aeroplane, the tank, and radio, provided new instruments for expansive policies in peace and in war. Third, the totalitarian regimes determinedly set out to use these instruments and pursue such policies.

The horrors of the war failed to persuade the people of all or even the majority of states that their interest in peace demanded a world order which must take precedence over their traditional national interests. The collective security system was ineffective because the Great Powers, both within and outside the League, were insufficiently determined in their support for it. Indeed, in terms of power politics, it proved pernicious. It utterly destroyed the possibility of flexible arrangements and it reduced the likelihood of action against an expanding nation since states directly interested, and hence ready to act, had to persuade and carry all those less directly concerned. The inter-war period witnessed an uneasy and inconclusive struggle between the new idea of collective security and the traditional one of the balance of power. From the very inception France tried to revive the latter, first by seeking a guarantee from the United States and Britain, then through a ring of alliances, the *cordon sanitaire* around the defeated *Reich*, then through the Locarno Agreements with Germany which ambiguously attempted to reconcile balance of power considerations with the collective security system, and finally by seeking an alliance with the Soviet Union.

When they looked back upon the failure of the League to prevent another war, the adherents both of the balance of power and of collective security agreed to one thing, that a stable order in the inter-war period was precluded by the lack of co-operation among the Great Powers—the recurrent differences between the French and the British, the isolationism of the United States, the long exclusion from international society of Germany and Russia, the lack of co-operation between the western Powers and Russia in the late thirties. Franklin Roosevelt at first envisaged a world order founded upon the idea of the Great Powers policing their spheres of influence, a system of loose world government which de Gaulle called permanent intervention. This did not appeal to the outsiders and anyway became impossible when the differences between the Soviet Union and the western Powers had become clear. Nevertheless, the idea of a Concert among the Great Powers served as the basis for the United Nations which attempted to establish a collective security force supplied mainly by these Powers and permitted regional security sub-systems. The collective security system did not materialize and only the latter survived.

Attempts to establish a new stable international order failed for the fundamental reason that the Great Powers that really mattered were reduced to the two Superpowers—the United States and the Soviet Union. Germany and Japan, the two defeated states, were temporarily eliminated; China was still very weak and France had not yet recovered from defeat; Britain was economically exhausted and it did not take many years to show that she could no longer rank as an equal. Independently of the fundamental ideological differences, disagreement between the two Superpowers was the logical consequence of their number; neither balance of power of the nineteenth-century type nor collective security could possibly work with only two protagonists.

The Post-war Bipolar System and Its Evolution

By the criteria previously suggested, the post-war system was highly revolutionary. Its composition was rapidly changing—the Superpowers were new to their status and responsibilities, the other Great Powers to their loss of status, the rapidly multiplying Asian and African states to their independence. The nuclear weapons and the ballistic missiles were new and terrifying instruments of destruction. Both Superpowers were governed by ideologies which rendered them intolerant in international relations: the expansive ambitions of communism were confronted by determined American opposition.

Until 1947 it was not clear that the world was becoming bipolar. It did not seem likely that the United States, unravaged by war and the only possessor of nuclear weapons, could be effectively challenged by the Soviet Union for some time at least. The antagonism between the Russians and the West soon deepened, but at first Britain, and not the United States, was the main opponent. It was quite possible that the Americans might withdraw into their traditional isolationism, as the Russians undoubtedly hoped they would. The Americans took the lead because the British proved incapable of bearing the financial strain of continuing to play the part of one of the Big Three. In rapid succession there came a British request for financial aid, an agreement to merge the British and the American zones in Germany, a withdrawal of British aid to Turkey and Greece. The watershed was the Truman Doctrine of March 1947, in which the President announced that the United States would take over British responsibilities in Greece and Turkey and that it would assist any country willing to resist communism. The cold war was joined.

Without attempting to apportion blame, the cold war may be regarded as a sparring match between the two giant states, a succession of moves and of countermoves. The process of involvement was gradual. The acute conflict between the United States and the Soviet Union was at first confined to Europe, but gradually spread to other continents—first Asia, then the Middle East, and finally also Latin America and Africa.

With a speed surprising to the West, the Russians developed nuclear weapons. Eventually the Soviet Union and the United States were not only threatening each other with nuclear extinction but were confronting each other everywhere; any change, in whatever part of the world, could affect the delicate equilibrium between them. This balance of power was quite different from the nineteenth-century one which had been based on the interplay among five Great Powers every one of whom had an interest in the survival of the others. Neither the Americans nor the Russians had a real interest in each other's survival since each would have found the world safer without the other. Apart from mutual fear, no powerful external restraints existed to prevent them from destroying each other. Admittedly, during the brief period of its nuclear monopoly, the United States did not act on the advice of the few extremist though logical advocates of a preventive war against the Soviet Union but simply used this monopoly to counter-balance Soviet preponderance in other, conventional weapons. Then the Russians developed their nuclear weapons, and the struggle resolved into the uneasy equilibrium of deterrence. In non-nuclear matters the balance remained precariously delicate since a light swing in favour of either side could sway the scales, perhaps irretrievably.

The United Nations idea of a Concert of the five Permanent Members of the Security Council was hopelessly out of date. The United Nations continued negotiations on collective security, disarmament and some other aspects of international order, although with rapidly decreasing prospects of success, but the emerging international order was clearly bipolar. In the cold war, states were inevitably attracted to one of the gravitational poles, either through the pressures of one Superpower or through fear of the other. The Soviet Union consolidated a ring of communist regimes around her western frontiers, and the United States successfully counteracted this move by supporting economically and militarily Western European States and by forming the NATO alliance. Since the NATO formula worked reasonably well in Europe, the Americans used it in other regions, supplying aid, establishing bases, concluding alliances. Two supra-national blocs seemed to be gradually emerging, the world was being sharply split into a communist part and what the Americans call 'the free world'.

For a short while the trend seemed more or less inexorable. There was no place for neutrals in the bipolar world, and both the Russians and the Americans regarded such states as India with suspicion; both applied the maxim that he who is not with us is against us. The bipolar character of the post-war world was revealed so suddenly that many people were blinded to other aspects of reality and became convinced that eventually the whole world would become divided into two antagonistic blocs facing each other—that the bipolar system would become fixed.

The prospects seemed poor, both for mankind faced with the danger of an atomic holocaust, and for the national states which seemed to be increasingly at the mercy of the Superpowers. The Soviet Union organized her empire rigidly and maintained sufficient troops in and near her 'satellites' to ensure compliance; the Americans used subtler pressures, but their series of alliances amounted to no less than counter-empire, less hierarchical but nevertheless clearly centring around the United States.

Then the forces of nationalism successfully asserted themselves. Instead of becoming tightly bipolar, the international order began to take a different direction. By the late forties consolidation within either bloc had not made much progress. Attempts to establish a 'Third Force' in Western Europe proved abortive, but in 1948 Yugoslavia successfully defied the Soviet Union. The Soviet-Yugoslav dispute was misleadingly clad in an ideological garb but was in fact an assertion of national ambitions against Soviet tutelage. Although this was not clear at the time, the dispute indicated that, after all, the Russians would not be able to consolidate their empire, and that consequently there was no prospect that such an empire and its American counterpart would swallow up the whole world.

Also the world outside the two opposing blocs refused to be moulded into tight bipolarity. Particularly important was the stand adopted by India. With the background of their traditional tolerance, their abhorrence of polarities and of militarism, the Indians chose to stay out of the two rival blocs. They, with the Yugoslavs, offered a pattern of behaviour for other emerging states in Asia and later also in Africa, who preferred to remain uncommitted. Nasser's Egypt and Nkrumah's Ghana became prominent among the newcomers. Gradually it became clear that one-third of mankind had decided against joining the two rival blocs, that a large portion of the globe would remain non-aligned.

In the fifties also the two opposing blocs loosened. Western European Powers, with a restored economy and revived spirit, were unwilling to follow American policies. That is why in 1956 Britain and France engaged in their abortive Suez expedition; de Gaulle's challenge to United States' leadership plunged NATO into a prolonged crisis. The nationalist riots in Hungary and Poland were a clear warning to the Russians that their satellites could not be subdued and exploited indefinitely and led to the loosening and liberalizing of the Eastern bloc. In Poland the process was halted but, in 1966, Rumania began to pursue an individual foreign policy, rejecting Soviet direction, and, in 1968, the Czechs defiantly liberalized their regime, eventually provoking the Russians into a large-scale military intervention. Perhaps most importantly, the Sino-Soviet rift which came into the open in 1958, gradually developed into a conflict, China becoming an adversary not only of the United States but also of the Soviet Union. Although she has been unsuccessful in securing followers and has been weakened by her prolonged Cultural Revolution, she is now an important individual factor in world politics and has the potential of a third Superpower.

Nor do the two Superpowers any longer retain a nuclear monopoly. Britain possesses and France and China are on the verge of producing operational nuclear weapons; several other countries could produce them within a fairly short time. Although these weapons could not possibly equal those of the United States and the Soviet Union and would not be likely to affect the balance of nuclear power between the two, they would endow their owners with much greater independence and flexibility in their foreign policies.

The outlines of the emerging new international system are still dim and fluctuating. It is possible to discern three blocs, the neutral one much looser than the other two, but it may be better to call the system polycentric since the centres of power are many and include not only blocs but also single states and the United Nations. Apparently the national states are not going to lose their importance. Not only the two Superpowers but other, less powerful states are playing a significant part in international relations. When it comes to purely regional issues, the weak African states working in concert have successfully prevailed against both Superpowers. They have adopted the General Assembly as their favourite forum and the United Nations is becoming a spokesman on their behalf. The future of the nuclear weapons is confused. While deterrence continues to keep nuclear danger at bay, the likelihood of the spread of nuclear weapons to further states and its implications remain uncertain.

The historical pattern of the balance of power cannot be adapted to modern realities and the blueprints for collective security seem unrealistic. The new international order is only in its formative stage and is likely to keep on changing. All we can do at the moment is to try to identify the main problems it is facing. Needless to say even this task can be performed only tentatively. Blinkered as we are by past experiences and by present problems, we may fail to identify what is going to be important in the future. However, the problems of today, such as the cold war, national clashes and anti-colonialism, and the striving for economic growth are obviously pressing and require discussion.

The Cold War and the Nuclear Dilemma

The term 'cold war' embraces all phenomena pertaining to the conflict between the communist and the democratic ideologies as well as their protagonists, the Soviet Union and the United States, and the two blocs led by these Superpowers, nuclear deterrence is an important strategic aspect of the situation. As the term most aptly expresses, it is neither peace nor war, a conflict which cannot be easily ended either by mutual compromise and accommodation or by the use of force, as conflicts were traditionally settled in the past.

The cold war presents such a serious problem for international relations because it combines two intractable elements: the clash between the hostile ideologies of communism and democracy, and between the two Superpowers who represent them. Each conflict alone would be serious. The ideological strife resembles in its intensity the religious strife of the sixteenth and seventeenth centuries which played havoc with the international society of the day even though a balance of power was possible because of the multiplicity of the units involved. Moreover, an international system centring around the two Superpowers would be inherently unstable even without an acute ideological difference. We have already discussed the gradual disappearance of bipolarity of power and the emergence of additional centres, and we must now consider the nature and prospects of the ideological conflict.

Both sides tend to regard their mutual differences in terms of black and white and have formed images of each other which obscure details and obstruct comparison. The differences between communism and liberal democracy are great but they do not exclude some important affinities, and rational analysis can indicate the possibilities for the abatement of the conflict. We cannot, of course, expect the antagonism to disappear because rational analysis shows that it is not fully warranted—the cold war involves too many ingrained emotions and prejudices. Nevertheless, the situation is not hopeless. While one generation in the seventeenth century was rent by religious strife, the next one managed to 'depoliticize' religion and to make possible the co-existence of Catholics and Protestants. Eventually nationalism became the main spiritual force, and we must bear in mind that nationalism is still very much alive.

Both communism and western democracy have a common origin in the ideas of the Enlightenment, of social progress based on rationalism. Both are democratic in the sense that their ultimate goals are the advancement of the individual, although they greatly differ in their methods of achieving this. While the West cherishes individual freedom, the essence of communism is to endow society with the power to impose a rational order even on unwilling individuals. The French Revolution left us the heritage of three principles: liberty, equality, and fraternity. It is an over-simplification but essentially true that the West has been pursuing the goal of political liberty and the communists that of economic equality, to the neglect of the other principles. The distinction is less valid today when economic equality has somewhat advanced in the West and political liberty in the East; fraternity, so far neglected on both sides, could conceivably provide an ultimate resolution of the ideological conflict. It is too early to forecast the outcome with confidence, but it seems that communism is gradually reforming its intolerant and proselytizing nature. Possibly economic growth and political stabilization will bring in their wake a further liberalization of the regime, and the hostility of western democracies to communism will change accordingly.

Ideologies have not become as all-embracing as religion was in the Middle Ages. It is conceivable that in the future the importance of ideological strife will be reduced by other conflicts already discernible: between the old centres of power and the Afro-Asian realm, between the industrialized and wealthy and the under-developed and poor, between the white and the coloured races. The established, prosperous, and white states may find sufficient solidarity in their stand against the remainder of the world to relegate their ideological differences to a politically unimportant role. Moreover, ideologies are not uniform even now. Western national variations such as exist between democracy of the American presidential and *laissez-faire* type and the British parliamentary welfare state, are now at least partly matched by the individual types of communism in Yugoslavia, China, or the Soviet Union. If the Czechs succeed in reviving their liberalized regime, the communist variety will equal that in the West.

In the twenty years of its duration the cold war has been the largest single factor in international relations. Several spectacular clashes, such as the Berlin Blockade in 1948, the Korean conflict in 1950, or the Cuban missile crisis in 1962 brought the world to the brink of a general war but, even during the greatest tension, restraint prevailed on both sides and the conflict remained limited. From the early fifties, the relations between the two Superpowers have been improving, although neither rapidly nor steadily. There are no clear signs of a real 'convergence' of the two diametrically opposed political systems although they share a number of important problems arising from their large-scale industrial organization and from their power positions. First, Stalin's death and, then, the dangerous Cuban missile crisis brought, however, a degree of *détente* which induces some observers to think that the cold war has come to an end. Indeed, although rivals in power politics and although ideologically divided, the two Superpowers share the dangers of the Chinese challenge and of nuclear proliferation and have managed to reach a series of written and tacit agreements.

Even if the cold war and the bipolarity gradually come to an end and the sharpness of the ideological conflict is attenuated, international society will still be faced with the problem of nuclear weapons. Both the Americans and the Russians have gradually accepted nuclear deterrence as a reasonably reliable means of maintaining a balance of power between themselves, but the balance is delicate. It involves colossal expenditure on the development and improvement of weapons and the danger of a nuclear war through escalation or accident. If the number of nuclear Powers multiplies, the possibility of a war will further increase. The problem of controlling nuclear weapons might easily survive the gradual dwindling of other problems of the cold war.

Anti-colonialism, Imperialism, Nationalism

Apart from the cold war, the major political stresses of the post-war world arose from anti-colonialism, from movements to over-throw the status of colonial dependence and to establish new states. Anti-colonialism operated sometimes independently from and sometimes in close connection with the East–West conflict. Britain freed India and other dependencies entirely on her own but the emancipation of the Belgian Congo became intermixed with the cold war. Although some explosive situations still exist in Southern Africa, the majority of the colonies have been emancipated. In more general terms, anti-colonialism can be included in the wider group of problems arising from the violent fluctuations of delimitation and identity of units; imperialism and nationalism belong to the same group.

Imperialism means the imposition of the rule of one group, foreign in some essential feature, over another, and is not confined to the colonial variety which characterized the nineteenth century and is disappearing now. The Russians and the Americans are quite justified in accusing each other of imperialism. The former exercise it over Central Asian people in the Soviet Union and through communist regimes imposed on unwilling people in eastern Europe, the latter less directly and effectively, through economic inducements and pressures.

The principle of national self-determination pronounced by Wilson in 1918 increased the incidence of clashes between nations

because the old-fashioned territorial disputes among states became aggravated by the complex issues of divided nations and
oppressed national minorities. In several respects the Second
World War resulted in a triumph of the principle of nationalism.
Through the cruel expedients of extermination and expulsion,
state boundaries in Europe began to approximate to the boundaries among nations. Only a few of the old-fashioned conflicts
linger, such as the Hungarian–Rumanian difference over Tran-
sylvania or the Austrian–Italian dispute regarding South Tyrol.
On the other hand, the cold war has established boundaries cutting right across the bodies politic of Germany, Korea, and Vietnam, and the discrepancy between national and bloc frontiers
may easily precipitate serious crises.

Nationalism has now loosened the two blocs. The Americans
give much more careful consideration to the independent policies
of their allies, while the Russians have been forced to relinquish
the economic exploitation and complete ideological and political
domination of their 'satellites'. Thus, by and large, nationalism
has been successful in withstanding imperialisms of all kinds. It
has been less successful in the newly arisen national states. These
have not yet had the time and conditions to consolidate, and are
usually torn between integrating forces of nationalism and opposing separatist forces. India has to contend with linguistic divisions, Pakistan with the separation between its eastern and
western parts; Burma with the hill-tribes and Ceylon with the
Indian minority; Indonesia has her troubles with the Outer
Islands, and the African states with their various tribes and regions. National self-determination is the generally accepted principle of state-formation but the boundaries of each nation are not
always clear and the tragic and futile struggles in the Belgian
Congo or in Nigeria may be repeated elsewhere, in an even more
acute form especially as the United Nations is unlikely to be in a
position to intervene.

To the danger of internal instability is added that of territorial
disputes within the Asian and the African continents. The new
states inherit colonial boundaries which rarely have ethnic or
economic justification. In some acute conflicts—in Kashmir between India and Pakistan or in Israel between the Arabs and the
Jews—force has been used but has brought no permanent solu-

tion. The boundaries simply follow the lines at which the con-
tending forces fought themselves to a standstill.

Economic Problems

Although immediately less urgent and dangerous than political
issues, in the longer run economic problems may become as serious as the former, excepting perhaps the nuclear dilemma. One
characteristic is common to the important economic problems—
they occur within the boundaries of states which cannot tackle
them single-handed. A serious challenge to the future international order is implicit in the question of how to cope with
these national problems which have become an international responsibility. Nearly all economic problems arise from the scarcity
of resources for meeting needs and all are interconnected—the
imbalance between population and food, the issues of economic
growth and industrialization, the scarcity of raw materials. The
bedevilling aspect of the situation is the seemingly inevitable
repetition of the rule that unto those who have shall be given.
Despite considerable national and international efforts to close it,
the gulf between the national incomes of the poor and the rich
countries is still growing. This is seen in an even more pronounced form when we compare the average *per capita* income of
their inhabitants, because the natural increase in the populations
of the poor countries is on the whole very much larger.

The most fundamental of the economic problems is the growing imbalance between the increase in population and in food
production of the poor countries, the Malthusian dilemma in
which they are caught. Until recently, fluctuating high death-
rates were effectively curbing the natural increase despite the consistently high birth-rates, but even slightly improved hygiene,
medical services, and food intake reduce mortality-rates, while
birth-rates do not come down nearly as rapidly. The result is an
explosive increase in numbers. A poor society growing at a rate of
2 per cent a year, or even more, must increase its national product
by an equivalent percentage in order not to become even poorer.
It takes quite strenuous running to stay in the same place. Food
production can be fairly easily expanded in such advanced countries as the United States, Canada, or Australia, but not in the
overpopulated poor countries where the uneducated peasants

cannot be easily taught improved methods of cultivation and where they are fully dependent on the vagaries of the climate.

The countries affected cannot possibly solve their problems by their own efforts. They rely on outside food supplies, at least in years of poor harvest, and on outside advice if they wish to introduce birth-control; they depend on outside help for industrialization, which is indispensable not only to increase national income but also as the only really effective long-run method to reduce high birth-rates through rural emigration to urban centres.

The last-mentioned expedient ties up with another economic issue, that of economic growth. Industrialized countries have reached a state of self-perpetuating growth because a fair proportion of national product is devoted each year to capital investment which produces an increase in this product higher than the increase of population. Poor or under-developed countries (they themselves prefer the name 'developing' countries) cannot find the capital they need at home. They produce little and cannot afford to save a large proportion of their product for investment because most of it must be used for essential needs of consumption. The only feasible solution lies in massive outside assistance together with an immediate reduction of birth-rates. Both have become enmeshed in the cold war. Economic growth is planned in the liberal Western, or the controlled communist way, while aid is given not according to economic need or economic promise but according to political considerations, to friends and benevolent neutrals. Even attitudes to birth-control are ideologically governed, the Americans advocating it and the Russians opposing it as a capitalist conspiracy to reduce the strength of the poor nations.

While on the whole the poor countries clearly depend on the rich ones, this is not necessarily so with regard to raw materials. All industrialized states, even the Superpowers, depend on the imports of at least some strategically important raw materials which they cannot produce. The competition for these materials is sure to increase immensely when more and more countries develop their industries. Even allowing for the incessant improvement in the exploration and exploitation of mineral deposits and for the invention of substitutes, some raw materials are certain to become very short in supply. The developing countries which happen to possess them will then be in an advantageous trading position. Again only an international solution of the scarcity seems possible, but at least the advantages this time would be on the side of the poorer countries, to some extent counterbalancing their weakness in other economic aspects.

7

The Instruments and Agencies of International Society

International Society and Its Members

IT HAS BEEN repeatedly stressed that international systems are more than the mechanical sums of interaction among their members, that they exhibit a certain structure and develop sets of norms for state behaviour. We shall now discuss how the historically evolved institutions of the contemporary international system cope with the issues confronting us.

International society does not include many units—only since the last war have they surpassed one hundred. Like many societies with few numbers it has not developed many specialized organs and instruments; in fact, until recently nearly all the activities carried out on its behalf were undertaken by its members, especially the Great Powers. However, harmony of interests between international society and the members acting for it cannot be assumed to exist in all situations. As has been argued, states act primarily in order to secure their national advantage and it is hard to imagine that they would ever refrain from pursuing it. Indeed, if we look into the operation of the Concert of Europe, we readily perceive how complex is the connection between individual and social roles; sometimes the suspicion arises that the presumably social role serves as a disguise for the pursuit of purely selfish interests.

While we recognize the confusion and hypocrisy implicit in the situation, we must bear in mind that international order depends upon the co-operation of the Great Powers and cannot possibly work if the vital interests of any of these Powers are adversely affected. Practical difficulties do arise but they can be solved in each single case. In theory the conundrum can be explained fairly easily. Actions against the vital interests of one's state cannot be in the interest of the system to which the state belongs, since the system would automatically become not worth while; on the other hand, once the preservation of international order in general is accepted as a vital national interest, the state may go quite far in overriding its more parochial interests and values.

Over the last hundred years, but mainly since the last war, there have arisen numerous agencies and institutions working for international society. They act simultaneously also for their individual state-members, and occasionally in the interests of a group of them or even of a single Power alone, but their major function is to act on behalf of international society. The new institutions express the evolution and sophistication of international politics just as division of labour and specialization express them in economics.

The operation of any international system is impeded by the small number of its members. Theoretically all states interact on the footing of sovereign equality, as if they were similar in most significant respects. In fact, they differ not only in power but also in their political systems and institutions, in the ideologies they profess, in the attitudes they adopt to the international order. They are pronouncedly individualistic and must be realistically accepted as being so. Failing large numbers, it is impossible to impose any far-reaching codes of behaviour which would rigidly apply to all, or to arrive at any significant statistical rules according to which such behaviour could be predicted. In a domestic society which numbers millions of individuals, norms of behaviour do not lose their general validity if they are occasionally infringed by a few; it is even possible to predict the frequency of such infringements. In international relations any statistical prediction of the probability of behaviour of units which are so different in some vital respects, would be very unreliable; moreover, violation of the norm by one single state may deprive it of its significance. What, for instance, would be the value of outlawing war or nuclear or any other weapons of mass-destruction if one Great Power refused to submit? The Superpowers and often also other Powers can be compared with the mighty feudal barons who could not be expected to accept all general norms of behaviour; not statistical forecasts but an analysis of their individual policies and attitudes is required for most purposes.

Hence, while it is possible to analyse an issue in a domestic society in abstract, without going into the identity of the parties, such analysis does not take us far in international relations. The identity of the states involved is as important as what is at stake. It is, for instance, clear that the Irish claim to Ulster creates an issue of quite a different nature than would a Soviet claim to a part of Finnish territory. An objection to a trivial infringement of diplomatic etiquette by one of the Superpowers can create an issue very much graver than the Iraqi claim to the whole of the territory of Kuwait. Weaker states have always found it difficult to deal with those more powerful. They have often been forced to seek the protection of greater Powers, and arrived at a position of dependence similar to that of the vassals in the feudal system; sometimes they were eventually absorbed by these Powers. Otherwise they formed combinations, like the Swiss or the American Federations, which reduced their inequality in relation to the more powerful states. Discrepancies have greatly increased today because the accumulation of power by the two Superpowers can scarcely be matched while, under the aegis of the United Nations, new states are coming into existence which could never have reached independence in the harsher climate of the pre-United Nations world.

Through their oscillations between periods of stability and revolution, over the last few centuries the relations between international society and its members have greatly increased both in scope and intensity. In every period of change they have to be re-arranged, and the more ramified and intensive they are, the more difficult does the task become. The problems of our own generation are considerably more involved than those following the French Revolution, not only because they are graver in themselves, but also because we have to deal with them in a much more complex framework.

Until now international societies have been subservient to their members, though not always to the same degree, depending on the type of structure. On the whole, since the war the two Superpowers could influence international order and were less subordinate to it than the several Great Powers participating in the balance of power in the nineteenth century. If, however, international society continues its evolution towards a polycentric type, its structure and the operation of its agencies will logically become more autonomous, and this seems to be happening already.

Norms Regulating the Behaviour of States

A society cannot operate without some normative social control of the behaviour of its members. When every member is a law unto himself, anarchy prevails, behaviour is unpredictable and social order cannot be maintained at all. International society differs from national societies in that it consists of states instead of individuals and is only loosely organized. Nevertheless analogies from a society of individuals are not unwarranted, provided they are not pushed too far and the differences are kept in mind.

A legal system is the most highly evolved form of expressing social order; but human behaviour is governed also by many other, non-legal norms, those of morality and of what is often called *mores*, such as custom, etiquette, or fashion. Some thinkers prefer to derive the highest of these norms, those of law and morality, from higher superhuman principles, but it is possible to explain them, together with the other norms, as the expression of social needs. Societies differ in the degree to which they permit variety in human behaviour and in the stress they put upon conformity. On the whole, the nature of the rules is governed by their social importance and is expressed in the type of sanction provided in cases of breach. If the social importance of the rules is slight, mild social disapproval suffices. For instance, a woman waiving the dictates of fashion may be slightly ridiculed or hampered in her social intercourse with more fashion-conscious individuals. If the dignity of an institution or occasion calls for the wearing of customary attire, anyone not so dressed may be refused admission—thus a woman in a sleeveless dress may not be allowed into an Italian church.

Social sanctions increase with the degree to which human behaviour seriously affects others. Some norms are incorporated in the law of the country and are enforced by central authority which tries to prevent their infringement and punishes their violation, but law cannot meet the whole range of socially undesirable possibilities. Hence law is supplemented by rules of morality which are not enforced the same way but are generally considered to be quite important. The sanctions for the violation of moral rules lie not only in individual conscience (which is assiduously trained in the desirable direction at home, at school, and in all social intercourse) but also in strong social pressures. If cruelty to children is to be avoided, the law can define only a limited number of punishable offences, but a person treating children cruelly, although not committing these offences, is likely, if discovered, to be condemned by his friends and neighbours. This too is a strong form of sanction.

These well-known and rather simple distinctions are mentioned here because they illuminate the more abstruse nature of the norms regulating the behaviour of states. As in domestic societies, the scope and nature of international norms are determined by those of social needs, but there is an important difference in the degree of social agreement which can be reached about them. By definition, domestic societies embody a considerable measure of fundamental social consent, without which they would not have come into being or would disintegrate. If such social consensus existed internationally, it would lead directly to world government. International order is based not so much on the consensus of its participants as on the physical fact that states exist and cannot escape from interaction. It is a world characterized mainly by the stark necessities of a Hobbesian society which has not yet evolved a fully articulated social contract.

Interaction among states is much less varied than interaction among individuals, and therefore the customs and conventions, the *mores*, of international society are not quite as complex and voluminous as those among individuals. As in a domestic society, the sanction for their infringement is social disapproval of suitable severity. In stable periods, such as that of the fairly homogeneous balance of power system, *mores* were generally observed but, in revolutionary periods, they are deliberately and flagrantly violated. A good illustration may be found in the determination shown by the bolshevik rulers of Russia, after they had come to power, to substitute direct relations with the people of other countries, and later with their communist parties, for traditional diplomatic relations. In a few years, when the dust had somewhat settled, the Russians reverted to the traditional forms of diplomacy, including ceremonial dress and titles, although they did not abandon their attempts at subversion.

The world is now rent by an ideological conflict and crowded by numerous new states with divergent cultural backgrounds; hence the traditions of the small homogeneous world of European diplomacy in the last century require substantial adaptation. Here the General Assembly of the United Nations plays a crucial role. Being a 'town meeting' of nearly all the peoples of the world, it compels them to make mutual adjustments in their behaviour and to accept a common code. Although much less homogeneous than its nineteenth-century predecessor, the international society of today can operate because states have become much more aware of the repercussions of their behaviour on others. To use a sociological term, from being predominantly self-centred they have now become 'other-oriented'. Needless to say, this does not mean that they are always willing to take the desires and susceptibilities of others into account.

International Morality

What makes the notion of international morality so ambiguous is that its meaning has never been clearly defined nor has there been agreement concerning the relation between the norms of individual and international morality. One school of thinkers, following Machiavelli, deny the existence of international morality altogether; others, like Kant, equate international morality with private morality; most thinkers accept the existence of international morality but differentiate between it and individual morality.

A realistic analysis of international relations cannot accept at their face-value the repeated protestations of statesmen of all countries that they are governed by moral rules. Clearly morality is often invoked under various names merely to provide a respectable garb for selfish state interests. It is a convenient common justification for claims which run counter to somebody else's legal rights. Since law is conservative and allows no claims in equity or way for revision, those demanding revision invariably invoke morality. The Versailles Peace Treaty was a binding legal agreement, but the Germans represented it as an immoral dictate of the victorious Powers determined to oppress them; it is similarly possible to question many legally established boundaries on the basis of national self-determination.

Nevertheless, it does not follow that Machiavelli was correct in rejecting the existence of international morality. Despite the lack of agreement as to its extent, international morality cannot be adapted to selfish ends in all circumstances. In our generation a claim for the revision of frontiers for the purpose of uniting a nation can be advanced and accepted as being morally justified, but, if made on grounds of economic necessity, such a claim would receive little sympathy from other states and from international public opinion and no statesman would think of advancing it. This is the first important reason why moral norms must be accepted as an influence upon the behaviour of states: this behaviour is perceived and evaluated in moral terms. Even if, in order to pursue a vital national interest, states sometimes ignore or flout international public opinion, they are generally interested in finding favour with it.

Second, the demarcation lines between domestic and international affairs and between states and individuals are not quite as sharp as they used to be. In the nineteenth century states alone had a standing in international law, and their treatment of individuals, provided these were their own subjects, was their own domestic affair. The excesses of Nazism have led to the extension of some rules of individual morality to the treatment of individuals by states. Human rights are now covered by a number of norms of behaviour some of which have hardened into law but most of which are limited to declarations and belong to the realm of morality.

Also the moral sentiments of statesmen as individuals must be remembered. It is safe to assume that, at least when their national interests are not seriously affected, they usually prefer to act in a way they consider moral rather than otherwise. This is particularly true about the practice of the United Kingdom and the United States. In the exceptional security these countries had enjoyed in the nineteenth century, they had the 'moral opportunity' of thinking in terms of morality and not, as continental statesmen usually did, in terms of necessity, of the *raison d'état*. On the other hand, it may be true, as Dr. Reinhold Niebuhr argues, that far from extending their moral rules to international politics, men tend to use these politics as an outlet for their immoral propensities—that they are moral men living in an immoral society.

The extreme Kantian proposition that international moral norms are identical with those governing individuals belongs to the realm of the ought. Ultimately everything probably should be reduced to the measure of man, but this does not alter the fact that states are not individuals and that the individuals acting on their behalf consider first their national advantage. Morality constitutes only a vague corrective to their behaviour, perhaps most concretely by providing advanced standards for the interpretation and evolution of international law. Beyond that, a vague obligation to meet the urgent needs of individuals, even if they belong to another state, may be on the way to becoming a generally accepted norm of international morality; in the case of large-scale natural calamities, when the national government has insufficient means to cope with the distress, other states which can afford it are expected to help, and a similar sense of responsibility for assisting economically backward countries is gradually growing, although it has not yet become generally accepted.

International Law

Just as the most important norms governing the behaviour of individuals are embodied in domestic, or as the lawyers call it 'municipal' law, so some norms governing the behaviour of states are embodied in international law. Even so, the identity of name does not indicate an identity of nature. International law operates in quite a different social context, without the foundations of an overwhelming social consensus and of a central authority which endows its rules with sanction. States differ from individuals in that they are not subject to law; international law is not a law above states but one between them. This is a situation so anomalous for a legal system that some professional lawyers altogether deny the legal character of international law, claiming that it lacks the distinctive characteristic of effective sanctions. Sovereign states and an international legal system of the same type as domestic legal systems are logically incompatible. Either the states are truly sovereign and recognize no superior, in which case there can be no legal rules binding them; or, if such rules exist, then states are not truly sovereign. The contradiction is resolved by the theory of consent which claims that the binding character of international legal norms is founded upon their acceptance by states, explicit or implied. Thus being bound by international law becomes a form of exercising sovereignty. In the classical definition of sovereignty in the Wimbledon case, the World Court emphatically declined '... to see in the conclusion of any Treaty by which a State undertakes to perform or refrain from performing a particular act an abandonment of sovereignty'.

Since international law is based upon such an uneasy compromise, it is not surprising that the evaluation of its significance ranges so widely. Some regard it a sham, while others claim that, if only given a chance by politicians, lawyers would draft a comprehensive code which would ensure peace upon earth. Neither view does full justice to the true nature of international law which tries to reconcile sovereign states and international order and is the expression both of state-sovereignty and of its limitations.

A sociological analysis of the norms of international law shows that they fall within three categories. First, there is what Georg Schwarzenberger calls the law of power. It consists of the rules helping to maintain the political framework, the existing hierarchies based upon power. Here belong norms ensuring the independence of states and non-interference in their domestic affairs, peace treaties, boundary agreements, alliances, etc. Then there is the law of reciprocity which regulates areas less vital for power-purposes where the states are willing to accommodate the interests of other states in order to obtain reciprocal benefits. This is the most numerous group of international norms, which covers many fields, for instance, diplomatic immunities and extradition, trade and communications, or limitations of warfare. Finally, there is an international community law, still at a rudimentary stage. Examples of it can be found in the regulation of the slave trade, or of international rivers, or in the standards of economic good neighbourliness in the General Agreement on Tariffs and Trade.[1]

Like all normative systems, international law incorporates certain principles of natural law, but a historical survey of its development shows that it has been formed more through state

[1] Georg Schwarzenberger, *Power Politics*, 3rd edn., 1964.

practice than through logical deduction. It is intimately linked with the balance of power system within which law performed the important task of laying down the rights and duties of states in relation to each other; most of its basic rules were developed in the fifteenth and sixteenth centuries when the system was coming into being.

International society is fully decentralized and possesses no legislature, but nevertheless it incorporates such a fundamental rule as *pacta sunt servanda* which enables states to develop the law through numerous reciprocal treaties. Some arrangements and clauses recur in the treaties regulating a given subject-matter and often serve as a basis for international customary law; this simply means that after a time they are taken for granted and need not be explicitly written into new treaties.

Another important consequence of the decentralization of international society is the absence of a central executive authority which could enforce the law. This, however, does not matter overmuch because this law does not attempt the unenforceable, does not impose on states rules liable to infringe their vital interests. States retain the ultimate right to use force and resort to war, and preserve an exclusive jurisdiction over domestic matters; despite some attempts to do so, intervention was never established as a legal institution. Although breaches of legal rules do not entail penal consequences, they are extremely rare: social pressures within international society usually prove a sufficient sanction, since all states wish to have the reputation of being law-abiding, which makes treaties with them more respected and desirable and, to some extent at least, shelters them from blackmail and hard bargaining to which less principled states can be subjected.

Within the balance of power system, international law was quite adequate and, with the partial break during the French Revolution and the Napoleonic Wars, it gradually developed into a fairly comprehensive system of rules. The general moderation and acceptance of the system made workable the law of power, despite its rudimentary nature; against the background of security, reciprocal interests gave rise to a rapid development of treaties, especially regarding commerce, while numerous conferences and a few permanent institutions began to extend the law of community.

When the balance of power system began to decline in the twentieth century, the many efforts to spread the 'rule of law', to develop international courts, to extend international law to the prohibition of the use of force, were bound to fail. Law is an expression of social order and is only marginally a formative element within it. The main reasons why these attempts failed was that the reformers confused the law of power with other groups of norms. The laws of reciprocity and community could develop and prosper only against the background of the security ensured by the operation of the balance of power. When this security disappeared and the law of power had to be fitted to a new international system, any attempts to extend community norms to the field of power were extremely naïve. Moreover, the legal system which had a European and Christian basis required adjustments to accommodate non-European and non-Christian states.

In the bipolar post-war world international law has lost much of its traditional meaning. The basic distinctions between domestic and international matters have disappeared and those between private and public acts have become blurred; many rules concerning territorial jurisdiction or the law of war and neutrality have been violated to the point of nullifying them; the new problems of nuclear weapons or outer space, or propaganda, cannot be readily solved. The conflicts in the bipolar world are so sharp that no security can be found within it; the relations between the two hostile blocs are so unsettled that the law of power cannot provide a reasonable background for reciprocity and co-operation, and in fact neither has reached its previous level. Simultaneously, the interaction within the blocs has become so intimate that in some respects it supersedes traditional international patterns and begins to resemble interaction within integrated political societies.

The sharp dichotomy of the bipolar world may now be resolving into a new polycentric order and, instead of becoming sharply differentiated into intra- and inter-bloc relations, international law is reverting to its more general function. However, it would be unrealistic to expect a return to the norms of the golden age of international law based upon the balance of power. There has been no break in the continuity of international law, as it is easier to adapt old concepts and institutions than to build up from scratch, but obviously the law of the new order will have to be a new kind of law. A large proportion of it is likely to take the form of the law of international institutions.

International Institutions

International institutions will be considered here only in their role of agencies of international order. Unfortunately this is too specialized and complex a field to allow more than the broadest outline of their historical development, structure, and activities.

People can save themselves much effort in personal life by developing routines to deal with recurring needs and situations. In social behaviour such routines take the form of institutions. In a broad sense the word institution includes such *ad hoc* arrangements as international conferences to settle a specific matter, but generally the name is reserved for establishments which operate continuously.

Most of the existing 1,200 international institutions are non-governmental, they combine national associations or individuals, and many of them represent relatively esoteric interests which have no direct bearing on politics. But even if singly these institutions exercise only a negligible impact on international relations, the thin strands, when woven together, constitute quite a strong rope. They represent so many individuals and organizations with trans-national affiliation that they form a link among the national states.

Out of the total number, about 150 institutions are inter-governmental, and include some which are politically important; only these will be discussed here. The term international organization is used interchangeably.

The first international institution, the Geodetic Union, was established only in 1864, and the subsequent proliferation of others clearly reflects an increased intensity in international relations. This was made possible by the exceptional stability of the balance of power order, but subsequent disturbance of this order did not spell the end of the existing institutions; on the contrary, it led to the establishment of additional ones, including those of greatest political significance, the League of Nations and the United Nations. History is important in explaining the nature of the institutions. They are not as closely connected with the balance of power as international law is. In fact, they largely represent twentieth-century forces and ideas which came into being after the balance óf power system had stopped functioning effectively.

Nevertheless, there is a close link between law and institutions. Some of the most important institutions have pronouncedly political objectives and are run by politicians and statesmen, but the drafting of their charters and their interpretation remain in the hands of lawyers. Legality, conformity with the constitution, is a necessary feature of any state policy which intends to win the support of the other members. Legal arguments can stretch interpretation of the constitution to great lengths, but there is a limit even to their flexibility, and the other members sit in judgement.

Here we come up against the fundamental difficulty of all international institutions, inherent in their dual role which theoretically need not, but actually sometimes does lead to incompatibilities. On the one hand, institutions pursue certain international objectives, work on behalf of international order. On the other, the member-states enter these institutions with the same interests as they had before, and expect them to be satisfied, or at least not infringed. Ideally there is a harmony of interests— co-operation within the institution improves the chances of satisfying the interests of states, thus compensating for incidental inconveniences—but this is not always the case. Britain had been a faithful though perhaps not very enthusiastic member of the United Nations, but has found it difficult to accept United Nations actions directly affecting British policies, such as the condemnation of the Suez expedition in 1956, or the violent and often uninformed and unrealistic attacks on British colonial policy.

In order to estimate the dual role of international institutions as instruments both of international order and of the national policies of the members, we should consider their place in the three realms of international politics dealt with by the laws of power, of reciprocity, and of community. As is the case with international law, institutions succeed in direct proportion to their distance from power politics: the less they affect the power-position of states, the more are these states likely to co-operate. Therefore immunities for diplomats were more acceptable than the outlawing of war; since mail is strategically less important than the telegraph and now the radio, the Universal Postal Union has been more successful than the International Tele-communications Union.

The lines between reciprocity and community cannot be sharply drawn because, once reciprocity among states reaches a certain level, it leads to the development of the rudiments of a community; for instance, reciprocal trade agreements have now established the good neighbour principle which has become in-corporated in the relevant international institution, the GATT. International organization has been both the result of certain common objectives and the agent for the development of com-munity ties. Where reciprocity has remained the rule, it serves as a convenient specialized channel for reciprocal arrangements.

Co-ordination and reciprocity were successfully carried over from the nineteenth century and further developed in the twentieth, when many new institutions were added to those few previously existing. The development of institutions concerned with power politics began only at the break of the century. The two Hague Conferences in 1899 and 1907 unsuccessfully attempted to provide a legal framework intended to limit the exercise of power and to facilitate the solution of disputes through non-violent means. The conventions concluded did not go very far, and the only institution established, the Permanent Court of Arbitration, was not in fact either permanent or a court, but merely a panel of names from which the parties could choose arbitrators for the settlement of any issue they might wish to submit. International institutions concerned with power politics arose only in the wake of the 1914–18 War, as a result of the bankruptcy of the old order based on the balance of power. Although the political relevance of the League of Nations in inter-war politics was not perhaps great, it is well worth while to return to the assumptions underlying its establishment, assump-tions which illuminate the nature of international organization although they are not widely accepted today.

The League of Nations and the United Nations in Historical Perspective

The League of Nations was conceived as a comprehensive in-stitution. In President Wilson's words, it was not to be 'merely a league to secure the peace of the world' but also 'a league that can be used for co-operation on any international matter'. The League was born out of the shock caused by the war and its main activities were to maintain peace. Hence its work in pursuing international co-operation on the lines developed in the nineteenth century did not become fully appreciated until its political activities had failed in the mid-thirties. Discussion of the non-political activities can be left to the following section; historical perspective depends mainly on the setting within the international system and the relations among the Great Powers of the period.

The framers of the Covenant of the League of Nations did not agree in their attitudes to the problems of peace. At the one extreme there was President Wilson, whose approach to international relations was evangelical, who wished to achieve through the League what another prominent statesman, General Smuts, called 'an inner transformation of international relations and institutions'. A concert of power was to end entangling alliances which he blamed for the war; a collective security system was to replace power politics. This was not, however, the attitude of Britain, who played the next most important part in the establishment of the League. The British regarded the League largely as an improved contemporary version of the 'Concert of Europe' which had so well served their national purposes in the nineteenth century. The French were concerned with guarantees against renewed German aggression. Hence they were particularly interested in the machinery of sanctions against a covenant-breaker, and their first draft included far-reaching provisions in this direction, including the establishment of a commander-in-chief with a permanent staff. Thus while Wilson conceived the League as an instrument of international order, the British and the French saw in it mainly a new instrument to serve their respective national interests and tried to mould it accordingly.

During the twenty years of its active existence, the League changed its character several times. When the Americans did not join it, rather unexpectedly the small neutral states became the spokesmen for collective security and the principles of international order. Their views, however, did not prevail since they were merely 'consumers of security'. The character of the League depended on the views of its Great Power members, those who would have borne the brunt of any collective action.

France and Britain deliberately pursued their respective national interests and therefore did not see eye to eye about the treatment of Germany and the role of the League. At first Germany and the other defeated countries were kept out, and the League amounted to a loose association of victors and neutrals directed against them in order to preserve the peace settlements. In the mid-twenties, in conformity with British views, Germany and the other defeated states were admitted in the vain expectation that they would co-operate from the inside in the maintenance of international order. After the danger of nazism had become clear and Hitler had left the League, the Soviet Union joined it and vainly tried to shape it into a fully fledged anti-Nazi alliance. For most of its existence the League stubbornly but futilely pursued general discussions about international order which will be analysed in the following section.

In 1945 the victors at least did not fundamentally disagree about the treatment of the defeated enemies. They formed the new international organization, the United Nations, as an association of 'peace-loving' nations directed against the potential aggressors, which in 1945 meant the defeated states. The United Nations was to be 'tougher' and 'more realistic' than its predecessor; the American President and Secretary of State made sure that this time neither the United States not the Soviet Union would stay out.

The Charter was signed in June 1945, but before the United Nations started its operations, it had become obsolete. The new nuclear weapons were first exploded in July and used with telling effect against Japan in August. The preponderance of the two Superpowers and the differences arising between them made unimportant the original agreements on the treatment of the defeated states—and, in any case, both sides soon deviated from their drastic provisions. Until 1947 the United Nations uneasily tried to bring the Charter into operation, working, as envisaged, mainly through the Security Council in which the Superpowers tried to reach agreement, usually in vain.

From 1948 the United Nations served, to a large extent, the ends of American national policy. The Russians could paralyse the Security Council by their power of veto, but the Americans made extensive use of the large majorities they could command in the General Assembly and shifted there the centre of political activities. The process culminated in 1950 when the Russians temporarily withdrew from all the organs of the organization. It is quite possible that they were preparing for a final withdrawal and were grooming a rival communist organization, the Partisans of Peace. However, when the Americans made use of their absence and secured United Nations support for their action against the communist North Koreans who had attacked American-protected South Korea in June 1950, the Russians immediately returned in order to impede further action in the matter and to safeguard themselves against such happenings in the future.

Between 1955 and 1957 the composition of the United Nations dramatically changed with the mass admission of Asian and African states. The United States, its European allies, and Latin American supporters, were no longer in the majority in the General Assembly. The new members were interested not in the cold war but in anti-colonialism; the Soviet Union supported them in accordance with her traditions, and secured their reciprocal support or at least neutrality. Since 1958 the United Nations has become increasingly identified with the Afro-Asian bloc and its aspirations, and as new African members are going to swell its ranks, it is likely to become even more so in the future.

Anti-colonialism, however, is bound to abate with the rapid emancipation of colonies, and the Afro-Asian members are likely to take an increasing interest in other aspects of international order. On the whole they are treating both Superpowers with suspicion and are refusing to side with either. They have been repeatedly urging them to refrain from behaviour endangering the peace of the world and to get on with disarmament. The Afro-Asian states are 'consumers of security', as had been the small states in the League, but their dependence on the Great Powers is not quite as great. They have, for instance, established the principle that United Nations intervention forces should consist only of contingents drawn from themselves and not from the Great Powers. The U.N. force in Cyprus included British troops only because they were available on the island and were indispensable for the constitution of the Force. So far international organization has been unable to make much progress towards a new type of international order mainly because its Great Power members could never agree. Although there is no guarantee that the smaller Powers will be capable of agreeing beyond their present anti-colonial objectives, it is at least not impossible.

We will turn now to the organization and the activities of the League of Nations and the United Nations which are of more than purely historical interest. The existing traditions may not be perpetuated by a United Nations in which the smaller Powers are preponderant, but they will serve at least as a starting point.

The Structure of International Institutions

World-wide international institutions centre round the United Nations with a membership of 127 states and with a wide competence in security, political, and non-political matters. Loosely co-ordinated and connected are thirteen Specialized Agencies which deal with more limited, technical aspects of world co-operation and generally have a more limited membership. Some of them, such as the Universal Postal and the International Telecommunications Unions (U.P.U. and I.T.U.) date back to the pre-United Nations days, but most of them, for example the Food and Agriculture Organization (F.A.O.) or United Nations Educational, Scientific, and Cultural Organization (UNESCO), or World Health Organization (W.H.O.) were established towards the end of the last war or since.

The structure of all these institutions is basically similar, although it shows some variations according to how relevant their activities are for power politics, and to the role played by the greater Powers. All the members are represented in some form of assembly, in the United Nations itself called the General Assembly. The principles of sovereign equality and of unanimity are sometimes slightly modified; in the predominantly technical International Bank and International Monetary Fund, voting is weighted by the amount of contributions made by the members; in the General Assembly of the United Nations, recommendations—which have no legally binding force—require only a two-thirds majority even on important matters.

The position of the Great Powers and main contributors is strengthened by another body, generally called a council, in which they are assured by the constitution or given in practice seats together with a small number of other members. The relations between the council and the assembly vary from institution to institution and, within them, in different periods, but in no case is the council an executive body acting on behalf of the assembly. The United Nations has three specialized councils—a Security Council of fifteen, with five Great Powers permanently represented (Britain, China, France, the Soviet Union, and the United States); an Economic and Social Council of twenty-seven, without permanent membership, and a Trusteeship Council in which countries administering and not administering trust territories are equally represented.

From the point of view of international order, extremely important organs of the institutions are their secretariats. Whereas the assemblies are based on the principles of sovereign equality of all members, and the councils, however imperfectly, endeavour to give some expression to power gradations, the secretariats act on behalf of the institution as a whole, as distinct from its individual members. Although he commands no state machinery, the Secretary-General of the United Nations is an internationally important personality. He cannot exercise much initiative on behalf of international order since the powerful members can successfully obstruct, but he can continue a policy once agreed upon by the organization and interpret his instructions with a fair degree of latitude.

The position of the Secretary-General acting on behalf of the United Nations as a whole, maintaining international order even against the national interest of powerful members or their blocs, is extremely precarious. He represents an organization which has no power or means except those provided by its members. The only tangible element of power which he can wield is international public opinion as expressed by these members. He must be always watchful in estimating what this opinion is and, even with the greatest care, he cannot avoid eventually antagonizing some members. This was the fate of Trygve Lie, the first Secretary-General of the United Nations, who accepted the American view that the communists had committed aggression in Korea and allowed full United Nations support for American action. This happened also to his more diplomatic successor, Dag Hammarskjöld, who pursued an active United Nations policy in the Congo, thwarting Soviet designs. Mr. Khrushchev's contention that no individual can be neutral is justified in the conditions of our generation, but his demand that the position of the Secretary-General should be split into a 'troika', a committee of three representatives of the three blocs (communist, western, and non-aligned) would have led to a complete paralysis of the organization. While the blocs would be able to exercise their veto, the organization could not conceivably do much for international order. Following the successful part played by the Secretary-General in the Cuban crisis in 1962, apparently the Russians accepted this.

Both in the League and in the United Nations, members retained their sovereign positions and the immunity of their domestic affairs from interference. However, this immunity in the United Nations was somewhat conditional, limited to matters 'essentially within the domestic jurisdiction' of the members, and the General Assembly gradually eroded it, the majority considering the ensuing disputes to be political rather than legal. Arguing that any domestic affair which effects international peace and security stops being essentially within domestic jurisdiction, the General Assembly has been freely discussing and making recommendations upon colonial matters, human rights, some aspects of the governmental systems of the members, all of which would have been considered entirely out of court by the Assembly of the League of Nations. Moreover, by Article 25 of the Charter, the members agreed 'to carry out the decisions of the Security Council in accordance with the present Charter'. This means that, provided the five Permanent Members concur, they, together with an additional four members of the Security Council, could impose far-reaching obligations on other states. The Permanent Members are immune because they can prevent an unacceptable decision by exercising their power of veto.

Maintenance of International Peace and Security and other Activities of Comprehensive International Institutions

The attempts to ensure the maintenance of international peace and security through suitable institutional means is best explained by a comparison with the maintenance of peace in a domestic society. In 1918, when the Covenant of the League was written, international society was still in an anarchic condition.

When negotiations and other methods for settling differences failed, the states resorted to the use of force and could be restrained only by force or its threat. While in domestic societies the widespread use of violence was ended by a degree of social consensus on the vesting of the monopoly of force in a central authority and by the establishment of such authority, only very radical thinkers could believe that these were feasible, at least within foreseeable time, in international society. The institutional devices did not go quite so far, but were an attempt to adapt some domestic institutions serving the maintenance of peace to the looser structure of international society.

One group of these institutional devices dealt with force. Its use by individual states was strongly circumscribed, or even prohibited; plans for collective security envisaged internationally administered sanctions against a peace-breaker; proposals for disarmament aimed at eliminating the danger of armament-races and the temptation to resort to war because armaments were abundant. Another group of devices imitated the domestic machinery for negotiations and adjudication of disputes, including the courts of law, and tried also to find some method for a peaceful change of legal relations to correspond with social changes. Finally, since satisfied states are more likely to remain peaceful than dissatisfied ones, various welfare measures, generally desirable for their own sake, were also aiming at peace.

The League of Nations Covenant circumscribed the legality of war. Members were allowed to resort to it only after certain prescribed procedures and 'cooling-off' periods had been adhered to. Moreover, the members expressly undertook to preserve each other's territorial integrity and political independence against external aggression (Art. 10). In the twenties, many international efforts went into 'closing the gaps' in the Covenant and outlawing war altogether. This was ostensibly achieved by the Briand-Kellogg Pact in 1928, which was signed by all states, with only insignificant exceptions. The signatories renounced war as an instrument of national policy and undertook not to seek the solution or settlement of disputes of whatever nature or origin by other than peaceful means. Although at the time this was not generally realized, war nevertheless remained lawful in at least five instances, notably in self-defence. The Charter of the United Nations, the signatories of which undertook to refrain from the use and threat of force in their international relations, explicitly authorized self-defence (Art. 2, para. 4, and Art. 51).

States could scarcely be expected to rely upon agreements alone, and the Covenant of the League therefore provided for collective sanctions against a covenant-breaker (Art. 16). There were to be diplomatic and economic sanctions which would be applied by the members automatically, simultaneously, and comprehensively, and optional military sanctions to be applied at the recommendation of the Council. The Charter introduced centralized sanctions, not differentiating between the non-military and the military ones. All sanctions were to be applied on the binding orders of the Security Council which was to have at its disposal a collective security force. Finally, both world wars ended in the disarmament of the defeated aggressors, and the Covenant provided for a general disarmament or limitation of armaments, while the Charter, having proposed a collective security force, limited itself to a provision for their regulation.

In the light of the historical record, all these attempts to circumscribe the use of force in international relations were unsuccessful. Plans did not materialize, agreements were hedged with escape clauses or interpreted so narrowly that they became meaningless, force was used in many minor conflicts and also on the largest scale in history in the Second World War. The activities of international institutions in this field largely amounted to statements of goals and aspirations. They were not, however, fully devoid of practical effects. Even the most limited form of United Nations intervention, such as inscribing an issue on an agenda and passing resolutions, is an influence, admittedly not an imperative one, which is taken into account by states contemplating the use of force. The United Nations was unable to stop some outbreaks of violence but effectively confined them and facilitated their termination.

'United Nations presence' is now an important international factor in many minor conflicts which do not directly affect one of the Superpowers. Sometimes a group of impartial observers is employed, as the U.N. Commission on India and Pakistan (U.N.C.I.P.); sometimes it is a body of trained military personnel used for supervision, most signally in Palestine (U.N. Truce Supervision Organization, U.N.T.S.O.); finally, it can be a proper military force. The first force of that type was used in the Suez zone to supervise the cease-fire and the withdrawal of the attacking forces (U.N. Emergency Force, U.N.E.F.). It was a brilliant improvisation due largely to the drive of Dag Hammarskjöld who recruited it among the few neutral states who had contingents to spare. Another, even larger force was used for various tasks in the Congo, including the politically explosive one of preserving the unity of the state. This force was involved in actual fighting and acquitted itself well. U.N. intervention forces are difficult to organize. They have to be recruited from states acceptable to the host country and they must be assured of finance. For a while the very survival of the organization was threatened because of the debts accumulated for the maintenance of the forces in the Middle East and in the Congo, to which the Soviet Union, France, and some other states refused to contribute. Even so, a small U.N. force facilitated the transition from Dutch to Indonesian rule in West Irian (New Guinea), another small force was sent to Yemen in 1963, and a larger one to Cyprus in 1964.

In the field of pacific settlement of disputes, international institutions not only added conciliation by their organs and judicial settlement by the World Court to the previously existing procedures, but also prodded and encouraged states to resort to pacific settlement instead of fighting. The achievement was, however, largely procedural. Many procedures exist, but resort to them does not ensure that settlement will be achieved. The standards by which international disputes are solved remain vague. The maintenance of peace without qualifications can easily lead to appeasement, to the satisfaction of aggressively minded states at the cost of weaker ones. 'Justice' is mentioned several times in the Charter, but is insufficiently articulated to provide a suitable criterion.

The trouble is that most disputes are not legal, not about the respective rights and duties of the parties, but political, aiming at the alteration of such rights and duties. Both the League and the United Nations were established in the aftermath of world wars primarily to maintain the *status quo*, the settlements arising from these wars. Both had only extremely vague provisions for procedures to be employed in revision of treaties and in peaceful change. The main 'peaceful change' (meaning one not involving a major war) in the inter-war period was the revision of the Peace Treaty of Versailles which took place outside the League. By contrast, the United Nations has partaken in much of the change since 1945, notably in accelerating progress towards colonial emancipation. Pressures by the United Nations have occasionally been great enough to force states to abandon their legal rights and to agree to a change but, needless to say, the influence of international organization both in the processes of conciliation and of peaceful change depends, to a very large extent, on the power of the parties; by and large the Superpowers are very much harder to persuade than smaller Powers.

The preamble of the Charter states the determination of its members 'to promote social progress and better standards of life in larger freedom' and for this end 'to employ international machinery for the promotion of economic and social advancement of all people'. This so-called 'functional co-operation' includes three distinct objectives. First of all, international co-operation in technical matters which had been dealt with by international bureaux already in the previous century has been maintained and extended to other fields, for instance, civil aviation and peaceful uses of atomic energy. Second, as a reaction against the excesses of totalitarianism and against the sufferings caused by the last war, humanitarian influences have found expression in many attempts to secure internationally the observance of human rights and the achievement of higher standards of social welfare. Third, since legitimate grievances could cause wars, economic and social progress could provide an additional way of preventing them.

When considered from each of these three angles, the record of international functional co-operation looks different. Technical co-operation has further advanced as in economic or cultural matters, or regarding outer space, but scarcely in accordance with the growing international interaction; where power considerations and selfish national interest are affected, progress has been painfully slow. The humanitarian influence has undoubtedly been established as part of international life. The very acceptance of the fact that the human rights of anybody, anywhere, is an international concern, and that the whole of international society is, at least to some vague extent, responsible for the economic and social welfare and progress of all its members, constitutes an important departure from the pre-war state of affairs.

Somewhat dubious is the assumption that the elimination of

economic and social grievances is likely to help in the prevention of war. It would be more convincing if conceivably such grievances could be fully eliminated, but in fact they can only be alleviated. There is no need for cynicism, for the humanitarian justification of international activities in this field is in itself sufficient, but it is rather illogical to assume that the hungry who are given half a loaf will be more peaceful. On the contrary, not being fully preoccupied with their struggle for existence and having more energy, they may become even more turbulent.

With its nearly universal membership, the United Nations is a meeting place of the states of the world and a symbol of world unity. The representatives of all states are forcibly reminded of the fact that their foreign policies and even their domestic affairs cannot be conducted exclusively in pursuit of selfish national aims. If the interests and feelings of other nations are affected, the issue comes under the discussion and scrutiny of the General Assembly. Every one of its members still pursues primarily an individual national interest, but the Assembly forces them to take other members into account as well. Many disputes and situations lose much of their potential danger when they receive publicity at an early stage, even though others thus become exacerbated.

When the General Assembly uneasily listens to acrimonious speeches and grapples with its overloaded agenda, perhaps it reflects a laborious but steady progress towards an international order which is gradually emerging from the countless permutations of the national interests voiced.

8
Prospects

FAILING AN IMMEDIATE SOLUTION for the urgent international problems confronting our generation, people tend to go to extremes. Some say in despair that the nuclear dilemma and the ideological and power conflicts between the United States and the communist state are insoluble, and that mankind is heading towards disaster. Others find the only possible solution in supranational organization, or world government, and expect them to materialize soon. The world can, of course, go either way, but it is more likely that it will go neither. The present position appears to us unbearable but it may continue for a long time until our problems are not perhaps solved but rather replaced by others. After all, religious wars were eventually fought to a standstill, and the French Revolution and the Napoleonic Wars did not prevent the restoration of the balance of power which ensured the most orderly century in Europe's history.

At the moment the ideological and the power conflicts involved in the cold war are grave but they may soon alter in character. There is a real gulf between western democracy and Soviet communism, but this gulf seems to be closing rather than broadening. One need not accept the Marxist doctrine that political superstructures are determined by their economic foundations to realize that the tremendous economic progress in the Soviet Union is likely to result in profound changes in the nature of communism; capitalism, too, has moved a long way from its classical *laissez faire* form. The power competition between the two Superpowers is unlikely to cease but both seem to be moving towards the conviction that a nuclear conflict is unthinkable and, beyond that, to the realization that they both share this conviction. Their nuclear armaments merely cancel each other; and thus new vistas open for competition in other non-military fields and for a growing measure of independence for their allies and for the neutrals. Bipolarity seems to be on the point of being transformed into a definite polycentric system.

What clues for the future arise from our analysis? The working hypothesis has been that mankind is loosely organized into an international society of sovereign states which rely mainly, although not exclusively, on power in their mutual relations. These states are represented by individuals holding certain official positions who determine state policies under the complex, often conflicting influences and pressures from their domestic and international environments. Inevitably, international society is subject to repeated crises and to the constant danger of war, although the growing co-operation among states gives some hope for an ultimate international order.

We are faced with a major crisis of the territorial sovereign state, the traditional unit of international society. No state is any longer self-sufficient or safe within its boundaries, all face a diminution of their sovereignty. The Superpowers are threatening each other with nuclear extermination and both are greatly overcommitted in their global politics, as are all the other greater Powers, some, like Britain and France, in the aftermath of their imperial past, others, like China or India, owing to the demands of economic development. Out of more than sixty new states established since the war, the majority are extremely poorly integrated and do not compare with the older, better-established states either in military, political, or economic power. The absurdity of the present system in which both giants and pygmies qualify for statehood is best exemplified by the tiny Pacific island of Nauru with a permanent population of some 2,000 which has been granted independence on expiration of the Trust Agreement.

For the time being we can expect the present division of mankind into states to retain much of its importance; as all the major colonies have become independent and have stabilized their frontiers, the violent fluctuations in the identity of states may come to a halt. Whether, in the long run, the division into states will continue must depend on the attitudes taken by the existing states to the future international order. The dust stirred up by the totalitarian excesses in the inter-war period, by the last war, and by the invention of nuclear weapons, has insufficiently settled for us to see where we are heading. There is general agreement that world order should guard us against a nuclear war and assist in economic development and in protection of human rights. There is no agreement about the role which will be played in this order by ideologies and by the various nations and states.

The desire to avoid a nuclear war is the most fundamental and intense common interest, shared by all states and men. At present, although precarious and generally distrusted, the 'balance of terror' is our sole means of protection. In this respect the main difference between the Superpowers and other states is that the Americans and the Russians fear each other, while others fear them both. Undoubtedly most human endeavour will be directed to finding a substitute for the 'balance of terror' or at least supplementing it with additional safeguards. Other nuclear Powers are likely to arise and further complicate the situation, but this danger may act as a spur to some early solution.

Less immediately urgent but in the long run equally important is the economic aspect of world order. It has now become generally accepted, both by the prospective recipients and donors, that the states which enjoy a high standard of living and a self-perpetuating economic growth, are under some vague obligation to assist the other, less fortunate states which constitute the majority of mankind. The exact implications of this new obligation have not yet been clarified and at the moment aid is given rather erratically, mainly according to political considerations. A new international order will have to evolve a code of rules about the amount, kind, provenance, and direction of aid, and also a code of obligations concerned with its use by the recipients. At the moment the explosive growth of the populations of Asia, Latin America, and Africa, puts the states of these continents into a stark Malthusian dilemma, but the technical means for tackling the problems internationally are readily available; improving methods of birth control and modern methods of economic planning; the great resources devoted to armaments, part of which could easily be diverted to other ends; nuclear energy for countries lacking other sources of power and cheap methods of evaporating sea-water for those lacking water; ideas about ocean-farming to increase protein supplies, etc. Economic aid arose partly from the cold war, from the desire to support allies and win neutrals, and it may further develop through the same incentive; with the abatement of the cold war it may dwindle, but it also could become properly internationalized.

Concern with human rights expresses the solidarity of mankind. At present, issues of human rights often serve the purposes of the cold war and of other political feuds, but if the ideals become firmly ingrained, their violation may rise to grave international reaction to the point of consolidating them as imperative rules of behaviour eminently suitable as a foundation of a humane international order. The civil war in Nigeria and the Russian intervention in Czechoslovakia may be indications to the contrary but may also be the last occurrences when international public opinion did not come fully to bear on events of this kind.

It is possible to discern the likely shape not only of the substantive concerns of the new world order but also of its agencies. It seems clear that we have departed from the traditions of the balance of power in which the Great Powers bore the responsibility for the operation of the system. Although the structure of the United Nations still perpetuates this notion through the institution of Permanent Members of the Security Council, and although the two Superpowers protect the world from a nuclear war through the 'balance of terror', the mutual and general distrust of the Superpowers is such that they cannot take part in any activities on behalf of international order except under strict supervision and control. This is largely true also of the other Great Powers, which, in the eyes of the Afro-Asians, are contaminated by their imperial past. In direct contradiction of the Charter, it is now an established ruling of the United Nations that its intervention forces do not accept contingents from the Permanent Members of the Security Council, although these Members are expected to make financial and other politically innocuous contributions, the exception in the case of the British forces on Cyprus merely proving the rule. Moreover, the clamour for aid without strings raised by the developing countries frustrates the political purposes of the donors, and may eventually end in some form of international control.

The new states, the Afro-Asian bloc in the United Nations, are not a satisfactory substitute. They are generally weak and unstable, and those few which have been contributing to United Nations intervention forces cannot possibly bear the full brunt of international responsibilities.

There is somewhat more promise in regional arrangements which embrace the sovereign states within determined geographical spheres. Admittedly, those of greatest moment have been used by the two Superpowers for cold war purposes, and those which do not include either Superpower, such as the Arab League or the Organization for African Unity, are still weak and ineffectual. Nevertheless, provided they can operate within a framework of international peace and security which preserves global peace, such regional arrangements may offer the most promising method for settling regional, local disputes.

Inevitably, the fundamental problem of international peace and security brings us back to the United Nations. The organization did not develop on the lines envisaged in the Charter, namely co-operation among the Great Powers, and nobody today regards it as a reliable guarantor of peace. Nevertheless, many people in all lands rest their hopes upon it. Of the Great Powers, only the United States has been a steadfast supporter of the organization, although now, when the majorities it commands in the General Assembly have started to wane, its support is becoming less enthusiastic. The Soviet Union is antagonistic, while France and, to a somewhat lesser extent, also Britain, resent the cavalier treatment of colonial matters. The staunchest supporters of the United Nations are the Afro-Asian states; and Dag Hammarskjöld logically concluded that the organization should work rather for the interests of this majority than for those of the Great Powers; this seems the most promising way of working for the future world order.

Although palpably powerless in the main spheres of influence of the Superpowers, the United Nations has become an indispensable agent for maintaining peace in Africa and in parts of Asia. Its future is still uncertain and it may, though this is unlikely, come to grief through financial difficulties or through obstruction by its major members. The successes of the United Nations have been limited to minor conflicts, but in dealing with them the Organization has developed procedures the potentialities of which are immense and incalculable. Moreover, it is the town meeting place of the world and the co-ordinating centre of functional co-operation. The demands of our age are so imperious and the facilities for meeting them, nationally or internationally, so slender, that it would be surprising if the institutional facilities which already exist in the United Nations were not used and further developed. So far, however, states are still pre-eminent and the future of the Organization depends upon the political will of the members.

Reading List

ARON, R., *Peace and War*, 1966. The most comprehensive philosophical and sociological analysis.

CARR, E. H., *The Twenty Year's Crisis, 1919–1939*, 2nd edn., 1946. The now classical analysis of the inter-war period.

CLAUDE, I. L., Jr., *Swords into Plowshares*, 3rd edn., 1964. A searching analysis of international organization.

DEUTSCH, K. W., *Nationalism and Social Communication*, 1962. *Nerves of Government*, 1963. Best application of the social communication approach.

FRANKEL, J., *The Making of Foreign Policy*, 1962. An analysis of decision-making.
International Politics: Conflict and Harmony, 1969. An analysis focusing on the two modes of state interaction.

GOODWIN, G. L., *Britain and the United Nations*, 1957. A full account of British attitudes to international order.

HERZ, J., *International Politics in the Nuclear Age*, 1959. An analysis centring on the crisis of the territorial state.

HOLSTI, K. J., *International Politics*. Most up-to-date sophisticated text-book.

HUDSON, G. F., *The Hard and Bitter Peace*, 1966. A concise analysis of world politics since 1945.

KAPLAN, M. A., *System and Process in International Relations*, 1957. First and most thorough application of system analysis.

MACHIAVELLI, *The Prince*. The classical work on power politics.

MORGENTHAU, H., *Politics Among Nations*, 4th edn., 1966. A leading American text-book based on the power-political approach.

NICOLSON, H., *Diplomacy*, 3rd edn., 1963. The classical treatment of the subject.

OPPENHEIM, L. F. L., *International Law: a Treatise*, 2 vols., 7th edn., 1952. The classical British treatment.

PALMER, R. R., *A History of the Modern World*, 2nd edn., 1963. A well interpreted history.

RAPOPORT, A., *Fights, Games and Debates*, 1960. A lucid application of the theory of games to International Relations.

SCHELLING, T. C., *The Strategy of Conflict*, 1960. An application of the bargaining theory and an analysis of the policy of deterrence.

SCHWARZENBERGER, G., *Power Politics*, 3rd edn., 1964. The only substantial British text-book.

Manual of International Law, 5th edn., 1967. A concise up-to-date text-book.

SNYDER, R. C. and others, *Foreign Policy Decision Making*, 1962. First, now classical, application of the decision-making approach.

THOMSON, D., *Europe Since Napoleon*, 1966. A fairly detailed one-volume history.

World History 1914–1968, 3rd edn., 1969. A brief introduction.

THUCYDIDES, *History of the Peloponnesian War*.

Periodicals and Surveys

BRITISH

Documents of International Affairs (annual).
International Affairs (quarterly).
Political Studies (quarterly).
Survey of International Affairs (annual).
Yearbook of World Affairs (annual).
World Today (monthly).

AMERICAN

American Political Science Review (quarterly).
Documents on American Foreign Relations (annual).
Foreign Affairs (quarterly).

International Organization (four monthly).
Journal of Conflict Resolution (quarterly).
The United States in World Affairs (annual).
World Politics (quarterly).

Index